The
Accidental
Law
Librarian

The
Accidental
Law
Librarian

Anthony Aycock

Information Today, Inc.
Medford, New Jersey

First Printing, 2013

The Accidental Law Librarian

Library of Congress Cataloging-in-Publication Data

Aycock, Anthony, 1973-
  The accidental law librarian / Anthony Aycock.
     pages cm
  Includes index.
  ISBN 978-1-57387-477-9
  1. Law libraries--United States--Handbooks, manuals, etc. 2. Law libraries--Reference services--United States. 3. Legal research--United States--Handbooks, manuals, etc. I. Title.
  Z675.L2A97 2013
  026'.3400973--dc23

                                                                    2013008051

Printed and bound in the United States of America

President and CEO: Thomas H. Hogan, Sr.
Editor-in-Chief and Publisher: John B. Bryans
VP Graphics and Production: M. Heide Dengler
Managing Editor: Amy M. Reeve
Editorial Assistant: Brandi Scardilli
Project Editor: Rachel Singer Gordon
Cover Designer: Ashlee Caruolo
Copyeditor: Beverly Michaels
Proofreader: Dorothy Pike
Indexer: Beth Palmer

www.infotoday.com

To Regina, Jessica, and Michaela.
Thank you for, well, everything.

Contents

Chapter 4: The Art of Hanging Loose(leaf) in an Uptight World 71

Chapter 5: The Big Two: Westlaw and LexisNexis 89

Chapter 6: Beyond the Big Two: Other Legal Databases 111

Chapter 7: Where's Waldo?: Public Information Searches for Law Librarians 135

Chapter 8: The Anxiety of the Men (and Women) Inside the Board Rooms 153

Chapter 9: Education and Resources 167

Chapter 10: The Future of Law Libraries . . 193

Appendix A: Patron Requests in Law Libraries 207

Appendix B: Library Business Case 217

About the Author 227

Index 229

About the Website
accidentallawlibrarian.wordpress.com

Go to accidentallawlibrarian.wordpress.com to find the companion blog for the year's hottest new book, *The Accidental Law Librarian*. ("Accidental" refers to the decision to work in a law library. The librarians themselves were not necessarily accidents.) On this site, you will find all the links discussed in this book plus others that I find that are ad rem, captivating, or worth a look. I will also add more thoughts on being a law librarian as well as an extra story or two. (Remind me to tell you about needing the October 14, 1998 episode of *Guiding Light* for a products liability case.)

If you, Constant Reader, want to share a good website or send a story from your nights in the law library trenches, please email me at pisancantos@yahoo.com. I will add them to the blog *a mensa et thoro* ("from bed and table," a term referring to legal separation, and also the two places where I am likely to update this blog).

Disclaimer

Neither the publisher nor the author makes any claim as to the results that may be obtained through the use of this webpage or of any of the internet resources it references or links to. Neither publisher nor author will be held liable for any results, or lack thereof, obtained by the use of this page or any of its links; for any third-party charges; or for any hardware, software, or other problems that may occur as the result of using it. This webpage is subject to change or discontinuation without notice at the discretion of the publisher and author.

Introduction

A few years ago, a staff member at the county public library called the law library where I was working. This was a small North Carolina county with a small library system, and she was calling from one of the branch libraries—the smallest branch, as I recall. This staff member had a patron with a legal question that she couldn't answer and wanted to know if she could send him my way.

"Sure," I said, and hung up, thinking I would probably never hear from the patron. When you work in a law library, referrals from public libraries are uncommon, for two main reasons. First, many people who learn they have to drive to *another* library to tell their story to *another* librarian simply decide to go home and look up the answer to their question online (not always a good decision, as you will see in this book). The other reason is that many public librarians are unfamiliar with the law libraries in their own area. So, I'll admit that I was surprised by the call I am telling you about.

Dealing With Dan

While I didn't expect the patron to show up, he did, later that same day. He looked about 60, with cotton-white hair and a weathered face, and he walked with the proto-shuffle of a lifelong day laborer. The guy—I'll call him Dan—did not appear to be a lawyer, doctor, professor, architect, stockbroker, artist, or any of the other educated classes. I figured that he probably just wanted to expunge a criminal record (a process spelled out in the North Carolina General Statutes) or locate documents from an old court case (something he would have to go to the courthouse for), and I steeled myself for a lengthy, incoherent encounter.

Dan surprised and shamed me by being well-spoken. He had inherited his father's house, which sat close to the highway. The Department of Transportation was preparing an offer for this property for a right-of-way, and he was going to meet with them in a few days. Dan wanted to know what questions to ask, what the offer would be based on, and what, if anything, he could do if he didn't like the offer. I heard him toss around words like *judgment* and *easement*. To a lawyer, these are terms of art. To the public, they can be as mysterious as Anatolian hieroglyphs.

When he finished his tale, I gave him my standard reply: "That's a huge research project." I say this about all but the simplest requests, not to deter patrons (though some need deterring, such as the ones who want to sue the President or Donald Trump or Satan[1]) but to prepare them. Most legal questions *are* complex, and truth is a mosaic of facts, not a spectrum. Dan looked at me, undeterred. "We have computers with internet access," I suggested, thinking he would be happy if he could sit down and bang keywords into Google. Dan, however, was doubtful: "Don't you have books, too?"

Well, yes, but it depended on what he wanted. He had said he was interested in cases. To most people, "cases" means copies of court documents: complaint, answer, judge's order, etc. Sometimes, what they really want to know is the amount of money paid by the loser of the case. This is called the *judgment*. There are books, journals, and newsletters that publish certain judgments, but these tend to be headline cases, ones where the plaintiff got, say, $10 million for having the wrong leg amputated. The average litigant needs run-of-the-mill judgments, which you can get only by visiting the courthouse where a case was tried and asking for a case by docket number. I told Dan this, and he furrowed his brow. "When

I lived in Florida," he said, "I was able to look up cases in law books."

He was talking about case reporters, which publish the rulings of cases on appeal (see Chapter 2). Now *I* was beginning to look like the ignorant one. "Those books contain court of appeals cases," I explained in a professorial tone. "They rule on procedural issues. They don't report on judgments or settlements." This is technically true, though every appellate ruling begins with a review of the facts at trial. Sometimes, this review mentions the monetary judgment. "Judges use the previous cases as guidelines," I went on, "but they aren't bound by them. They can still do what they want."

Again, technically true, though there are exceptions. But I was beyond managing Dan's expectations. I was even beyond rendering genuine help. Before Dan had opened his mouth, I had taken him for a rube, someone I could wow with legal jargon and a scholarly air. He had turned out to be pretty smart. Worse, he hadn't taken my hints to go away, which was bugging me. In response to my harangue on appellate cases, he used the word *precedent*, and it fit into his sentence like a diamond pick in a pin-tumbler lock. So this guy knew about precedent. What else did he know? And when would this encounter be over?

At that moment, I had a revelation. Instead of using my expertise as leverage to answer Dan's questions, I had made it a buffer between the questions and me. I had been condescending, judgmental, and, worst of all, deaf. Dan had told me plenty about what he needed, and I had responded with what I had wanted to give him: nothing. I was a lousy librarian—so far. But there was still time for an about-face, and I decided to do one.

Turning to my computer, I did a Google search for *right of way laws in nc*. (He had used the term *right of way*—that much I had heard.) This led me to the Right of Way Division of the North Carolina Department of Transportation website. The division is responsible for buying up the lands and rights of way necessary for construction and improvement of all North Carolina roads—interstate, U.S. and state routes, and secondary roadways. The Negotiations Unit, a segment of the Right of Way Division, contacts property owners affected by proposed roadways to purchase rights of way, or sometimes the whole property, if it will be needed for materials storage or environmental mitigation for a nearby project. To do this, the unit researches property records, requests appraisals or condemnations, and prepares fee simple deeds and deeds of release. Most of all, and most crucial to Dan, it negotiates personally with individual property owners.

As I was skimming the page, Dan, who couldn't see my screen, mused, "You know, I think the people who are coming are actually from the"—pause, think, got it!—"Right of Way Division." Okay, Dan, okay. I had had my change of heart. Would his next trick be an eminent domain argument before the Supreme Court? Getting up from my chair, I walked to the North Carolina General Statutes. Dan followed. I looked up *right of way* in the index but didn't see anything useful. Then I tried the two-volume *Webster's Real Estate Law in North Carolina*, again looking up *right of way* in the index. Still nothing. Then I had another revelation. Dan had used the word *easement* when he first narrated his story. Flipping to *easement* in the index, I saw multiple subheadings, all from Chapter 15. Bingo.

Wanting to give Dan a second source, I turned to *Strong's North Carolina Index*, which, despite its name, is not an index. It is instead an encyclopedia of North Carolina law. Topics are arranged alphabetically as in *Grolier's*, *World Book*, or any encyclopedia. I showed Dan the article on easements, which, in conjunction with the *Webster's* information, made him grateful, so grateful. This is what I should have done all along.

Building the Background

How was I able to help Dan find the information he wanted? How did I recognize the term *easement*, know about *Webster's* and *Strong's*, and give my misguided (but still accurate) explanations of judgments and appeals cases? My answers came from my 10 years' experience in various law libraries, of course. But, what about an inexperienced person? What about a circulation desk staffer, or library school intern, or brand-new graduate? What about a long-serving public librarian who has never, for one reason or another, had much chance to deliver legal reference? In law firms or corporate legal departments, library staff may have no relevant training. At one firm, my predecessor had been a reassigned paralegal. Before her, it was a retired schoolteacher. What would these folks have done to steer Dan in the right direction?

I was in that very position in January 2001, a month after finishing my MLIS at the University of South Carolina. Throughout my final semester, I had applied for library jobs all over the country. The response? Silence. December graduation came and went, and with a family to support, I brought my job search home, applying for anything, even restaurant management, which I had done years before. One of the jobs I applied for was a litigation assistant position with a 100-plus attorney law firm with several South Carolina offices, including downtown Columbia, where I lived. I knew nothing about the law or law firms, but the newspaper description had mentioned research, which I knew I could do. I landed an interview with the firm's human resources manager—an interview, but not the job.

A week or so later, someone else from the firm called me. She said she was the firm's librarian—I didn't even know law firms had libraries—and that she knew I had recently interviewed for the litigation assistant job. Would I like to interview again, this time for a library clerk position that had just become available? Why, yes, I would.

The next day, I pulled my black suit pants out of the laundry, drove downtown a second time, sat in a leather office chair that cost triple my monthly car payment, interviewed, and got the job. Just like that, I was working in a law library. And I still knew nothing about the law. Working with legal materials every day, of course, I got the hang of them after a while. That is, I could look up a case or statute, or find a specific section of a book, or do simple database searches. In-depth research, of course, took me a lot longer to master.

In her foreword to *Law Librarianship in the Twenty-First Century*, Vicki Gregory notes that law librarianship is an important field, with its own vocabulary and an unparalleled print heritage. It is also unique in that it has a dual goal: serving legal specialists (lawyers, paralegals, judges) as well as the public. "We are all," Gregory says, "affected by and bound by the law." Certain cities have dedicated public law libraries, though these are being shuttered all across the U.S. (see Chapter 10). In the rest of the country, the public, as well as solo or small-firm attorneys, has to rely on public libraries.[2] Because they aren't immersed in legal practice as I had to be, most public librarians never develop any real expertise. Collection managers don't understand the intricacies of legal publishing, which limits their ability to develop good legal collections. Law books are dense and confounding, and reference librarians lack the skills to help people navigate them. Besides, public libraries are scared to death of the unauthorized practice of law— an unfounded fear, as I explain in Chapter 3. Academic law librarians (i.e., those who work in law schools) often have law degrees as well as library degrees. Law firm librarians occasionally have both (my boss at that first law firm didn't; my boss at a later firm did). Public librarians, in many cases, have not had even one class in law librarianship.

Historically, library schools have ignored the discipline of law. Law librarians were just retired or nonpracticing lawyers, or they were secretaries or apprentices. Any legal expertise possessed by librarians was picked up in the field (like me) or by going to law school. When law libraries were confined to academe, this was OK. But the law is everywhere now, and more people than ever need help researching it. There aren't enough dual-degreed librarians to go around. Law librarianship, once a detour in the study of law, is now a destination. Yet courses in law librarianship or legal reference are not even offered in some MLIS programs and are scarcely supported in others. My alma mater had such a course, but it was not offered once the whole time I was there. Later, I taught a semester of legal reference at another school. The class was small but fun, and the students seemed to enjoy it. When I offered to teach a second semester, however, the dean failed to return my calls. Repeatedly.

Self-study doesn't provide many more options. Textbooks on legal research and writing are legion, and I discuss a few in Chapter 9. Research techniques, however, are only one tool in the law librarian's workshop. Collection management, business development, electronic licenses, legal history, database searching—these and other skills are scattered among law librarian blogs, journals, and other literature. Deborah Panella and Ellis Mount's *Basics of Law Librarianship* was the last introductory book, and it was published in 1991. Others since then have focused on a single aspect or type of law library (see Chapter 9 for a discussion of some of these).

The Accidental Law Librarian is the first comprehensive, non-scholarly book on law libraries in 20-plus years. It is not focused on academic law librarians, who, as I have noted, often have formal training in the law. Rather, like other books in Information Today, Inc.'s Accidental Librarian series, it is a resource for people thrust into the law librarian role. From legal research basics to the needs of legal information seekers, from database licensing to database use, from the history of legal publishing to the future of law libraries, *The Accidental Law Librarian* is the book to help public librarians build better collections and deliver accurate, worry-free service. It is the book that law firm administrators and library trustees need to read as they consider the fate of the law libraries entrusted to them. It is the book I wish I had had on my first day at that first law firm, and it is the book to help you when Dan the Day Laborer, or someone like him, shows up at your desk with all the weight of the world on his—and your—shoulders.

Endnotes

1. The Prince of Darkness has, in fact, been a defendant in federal court. See *United States ex. rel. Gerald Mayo v. Satan and His Staff*, 54 F.R.D. 282 (W.D. Pa. 1971).
2. In this book, I use the terms *public libraries* and *public librarians* in reference to all libraries open to the public, no matter how they are organized and funded.

Chapter 1

Legal Publishing, or What Are All Those Books on *Law and Order*?

This chapter gives an overview of legal publications and is intended specifically for new librarians who work in law firms and public law libraries. *Any* librarian, however, will benefit from this discussion. In cities where there is no public law library, public or academic librarians tend to receive law-related questions. They should know the basics of legal materials for collection development (covered later in this chapter) and for reference service (see Chapter 3).

This collection development discussion, though, will focus on law firm and public law libraries rather than on academic law libraries, due to their specialized needs. Law professors, as scholars, need access to historical and interdisciplinary materials that would be of little use to practicing attorneys. Most academic law librarians, moreover, have law degrees (see Chapter 9), meaning they are already familiar with the basics I discuss in this chapter. Finally, there are already plenty of resources on academic law library collection development. Two of the best are Gordon Russell and Michael Chiorazzi's *Law Library Collection Development in the Digital Age* (see Chapter 9) and *Legal Research and Law Library Management* by Julius Marke, Richard Sloane, and Linda Ryan.

For law firm and public law librarians, there are two broad categories of legal materials: primary and secondary.

Primary Sources

Primary sources are what most people mean by "the law." These are "the sum total of the rules governing individual and group behavior that are enforceable in court."[1] Law librarians deal with three major categories of primary sources.

Statutes

Statutes are legislation enacted by an elected body—the U.S. Congress, for example, or a state legislature. Congress has its own legislative process, as does each state. The chart provided at www.dailyinfographic.com/how-our-laws-are-made-infographic illustrates the U.S. Congress legislative process; the graphic provided at www.ncleg.net/ncgainfo/bill-law/bill-law.gif illustrates the North Carolina legislative process.

Cases

A *case*, also called an *opinion* or *decision*, is a written ruling issued by a court on a specific matter. Judges are bound in their rulings by how similar cases in the same jurisdiction were decided in the past. This principle—as Dan, the patron mentioned in the Introduction, knew so well—is called *precedent*, and it is the foundation of the American common law system.[2] Cases may be published or unpublished, and if you have watched *Law and Order* on television, then you have seen books of published cases—the tan hardcover volumes with black and red stripes. (If you haven't noticed these before, look for them. They often appear in bookcases in hallways, courtrooms, or the district attorney's office.)

Administrative Law

Administrative law refers to the regulations and decisions made by administrative agencies, both at the federal and state level. As I discuss in Chapter 2, regulations are like statutes, and agency decisions are analogous to court cases; agency documents carry the same force of law. Agencies are created by statute and charged with regulating an area of society. The U.S. Food and Drug Administration, for example, ensures public safety by requiring drug companies to adhere to testing and reporting standards. Federal agencies report ultimately to the president, state agencies to the governor.

These agencies touch nearly everything we do as citizens. As a North Carolina resident, I pay employment taxes to the Internal Revenue Service and the North Carolina Department of Revenue, have money withheld by the Social Security Administration, get my driver's license from the North Carolina Department of Motor Vehicles, drive on bridges designed by the Army Corps of Engineers, vacation in parks managed by the North Carolina Wildlife Resources Commission, ride in elevators inspected by the North Carolina Department of Labor, fly in planes regulated by the Federal Aviation Administration, send packages through the U.S. Post Office, and drift to sleep on a mattress bearing a tag required by the Consumer Product Safety Commission.[3]

Secondary Sources

Secondary sources are materials that discuss, explain, analyze, and critique the law. They are resources about the law, not the law itself. Remember the two sources I showed to Dan, *Strong's North Carolina Index* and *Webster's Real Estate Law in North Carolina*? Those were both secondary sources. I used them to help me find primary sources relevant to Dan's research.

For more about primary and secondary sources, see Chapter 2.[4]

History of Legal Publishing

To understand legal publications, it helps to know a bit about where they came from. English legal publishing got its start in the

1480s, when William de Machlinia printed the *English Year Books*, handwritten law reports dating back to the 13th century. Lawyers at this time, as part of their professional training, sat in court and took notes on pleadings (i.e., the claims and defenses by parties to a lawsuit) as well as dialogue between lawyers and judges and any statements of law. They did not record every case, and the recordings they made typically lacked the names of the parties or the outcomes of the cases. Still, the *Year Books* are valuable because they record the "earliest stages of development of procedure, argument, and doctrine in the common law tradition."[5] Later, the publisher Richard Pynson released *Statham's Abridgment*, a collection of summaries of cases from the *Year Books*, which were organized under alphabetical subject headings. It was the ancestor of the modern-day West digest (see Chapter 2).

Machlinia also gave us the first book of statutes, the *Nova Statuta*, published in 1485 but dating back to 1327. More collections of statutes and cases appeared during the 16th and 17th centuries, as did treatises (big, explanatory texts about the law), legal manuals and dictionaries, formbooks, and other abridgments modeled on *Stratham's*. All these were secondary sources. When the *Year Books* were discontinued in 1535, other individuals took up the task of publishing cases, naming the works after themselves (e.g., *Hutton's Common Pleas Reports*). This practice continued into the 19th century in England and the U.S.

Of the leading treatises, the most influential was William Blackstone's *Commentaries on the Laws of England*.[6] Unlike most European nations, whose Roman-inspired legal systems were heavy on statutes and codes, England had a common law system, relying on actual cases to establish precedents. Common law has more room for interpretation, which explains the need for treatises. Blackstone's was the most readable and therefore the most influential, inspiring James Kent's *Commentaries on the American Law* in 1826.

After its political break from England in 1787, the new United States began to develop its own system of law. In the colonial era, printers had turned out legal materials in addition to their other commissions. However, in the 19th century, specialized legal publishers emerged. "Official" publications called *case reporters*, published at state rather than private expense, replaced the patchwork of named reporters like *Hutton's* that had followed the colonists from England. *Reporter* is still the term for collections of cases, whether published by the federal or state government or by a commercial publisher such as West (see Chapter 2).

States also began publishing statutes, and as legal training moved from apprenticeships to law schools in the late 1800s, textbooks of law began to appear. One type of text was the *casebook*, a collection of cases, condensed to their essentials, on a particular topic. Casebooks, the creation of Christopher Columbus Langdell (dean of Harvard Law School from 1870 until 1895), remain the primary texts used in law schools today.[7]

John B. West Changes the Game

Every industry has its game changers. Henry Ford took the automobile, a plaything of the rich, and put it in nearly every home in America. Ray Kroc bought a little hamburger joint from the McDonald brothers and turned it into the world's largest restaurant chain. Bill Gates and Steve Jobs oversaw a new era in personal computing. In legal publishing, the game changer was John B. West. In the 1870s, case reporting was a diffuse, unsophisticated, and maddening business. State court clerks often waited as much as a year before publishing court decisions, which by then, due to new precedents, were already outdated. Moreover, attorneys west of the Mississippi had trouble getting legal books from East Coast publishers, making it hard for them to do research for their cases.[8]

John West changed all that. A bookseller for Minnesota-based publisher D.D. Merrill, he knew the complaints of his attorney customers. In 1872, he quit Merrill and established his own firm to focus on the local bar. He created a line of legal forms, reprinted hard-to-find treatises, and produced a much-needed index to the Minnesota statutes.[9] In 1876, West and his brother Horatio released a weekly journal called *The Syllabi*. Each issue contained "the syllabus (prepared by the Judge, writing the opinion) of each decision of the Supreme Court of Minnesota, as soon after the same is filed as may be practicable, accompanied, when desirable to a proper understanding of the points decided, with an abstract of the case itself, and when the decision is one of general interest and importance, with the full opinion of the Court."[10] It also published important decisions of lower Minnesota courts and federal courts in the state.

The Syllabi grew into the *North Western Reporter*. Other regional reporters followed, and in 1887, West turned his attention to what he called "the American Digest Classification Scheme."[11] Basically, this was an index of American law using some 200 topics that were further divided into "key numbers," each representing one legal concept, or point of law. Each case, regardless of jurisdiction, was printed with the key numbers corresponding to its points of law. This meant that, for the first time ever, attorneys could find cases by *subject*.

More than a century later, West[12] publishes cases from every federal and state jurisdiction, indexing them with this same topic and key number system. A few states publish their own case reporters, but most have outsourced the job to West, as has the federal government, which publishes its own version of U.S. Supreme Court cases, but not those of the lower courts. In addition to West, other major legal publishers emerged in the late 19th and early 20th centuries. These included:

- Callaghan and Company (1863), publishing treatises and practice guides

- Shepard's (1873), the leading citator, or list of authorities that cite, or discuss, a particular case (see Chapter 2)

- Matthew Bender (1887), another treatise publisher

- Michie (1897), publishing state statutes

- Commerce Clearing House (1913), publisher of the first looseleaf service (for more on looseleafs, see Chapter 4)

- Bureau of National Affairs (1933)

- Practising Law Institute (1933)

- Research Institute of America (1935), a major publisher of U.S. tax materials

- Warren, Gorham & Lamont (1961)

- Prentice Hall Law & Business (1973)

- John Wiley Law Publications (1983)[13]

Modern Legal Publishing

In 1977, according to one account, "there were 23 fairly substantial independent legal publishers."[14] By 2006, three conglomerates, not-so-affectionately known as "The Big Three"—Thomson West, owned by Canada's Thomson Corporation; Reed Elsevier, a Dutch company; and Wolters Kluwer, based in the Netherlands—had bought up 80 percent of the industry.[15] Therefore, just four publishers—The Big Three and U.S. publisher Bureau of National Affairs (BNA)—had control of 97 percent of the law-related market in the U.S.

The industry, however, is still consolidating. For years, there has been speculation that Reed Elsevier and Wolters Kluwer would merge, creating the world's leading supplier of scientific and professional information. Such a merger "has been seen by some analysts as the only way for the two companies to achieve the critical mass necessary to compete effectively with Thomson Reuters."[16] Even BNA, touting itself for years as the only independent U.S. legal publisher, is now owned by Bloomberg. Table 1.1 provides a breakdown of The Big Three's products.

Table 1.1 A Breakdown of The Big Three's Products

Name	Law-Related Imprints	Major Products
Thomson Reuters	West Publishing Callaghan & Company Clark Boardman Warren, Gorham & Lamont Lawyers Cooperative RIA Sweet & Maxwell Shepard's (treatises) Foundation Press Findlaw Harrison Company Dialog GlasserLegalWorks Hildebrandt International Global Securities Information, Inc.	*National Reporter System* *United States Code Annotated* Most state statutes West digests Largest number of treatises Westlaw KeyCite (does not exist in print) Hornbooks Nutshell series *Black's Law Dictionary* Findlaw.com (free public website) CLEAR public records database

Reed Elsevier	Lexis
	R.R. Bowker
	Martindale-Hubbell
	Butterworths
	Michie
	Shepard's
	Matthew Bender
	Mealey's Publications
	Courtlink
	Anderson Publishing
		U.S. Supreme Court Reports,
		  Lawyers Edition
		United States Code Service
		Most state statutes (some same as
		  West but with different
		  annotations)
		Substantial number of treatises
		Lexis.com
		Shepard's Citations (still published
		  in print)
		Matthew Bender treatises
		Mealey's Litigation Reports
		Accurint
		Lexisone.com (free public website)
		Courtlink public records database

Wolters Kluwer	Aspen Law & Business CCH Little, Brown (treatises) Wiley Law	CCH looseleafs CCH.com Substantial number of treatises Aspen paralegal textbooks *Glannon Guides* *CrunchTime* *Emanuel Law Outlines* *Examples & Explanations* series Loislaw.com

Other publishers that law librarians often interact with include the following:

- BNA publishes hundreds of newsletters in dozens of practice areas (see Chapter 4) and also publishes some treatises.

- The Dolan Company (www.thedolancompany.com) publishes over 50 state business and legal newspapers.

- Some individual states, as I mentioned, publish their own appellate cases, which are not indexed by West's topic and key number system. No state publishes its own statutes, instead relying on West or Lexis to publish them.

- James Publishing has litigation-oriented titles centering on state court trial issues.

- Jones McClure offers large-market state jurisdiction treatises (e.g., Texas and California) with some federal treatises.

- The U.S. Government Printing Office prints the *U.S. Code* and *U.S. Reports* (i.e., Supreme Court cases). The statutes are not annotated, and the cases are not indexed (see Chapter 2 for the importance of these features).

Price Increases

The biggest effect of this consolidation of legal publishers on libraries has been hefty price increases. Multivolume treatises in particular have gone up significantly. According to one report, after Thomson acquired Lawyer's Cooperative in 1989, prices shot up at "about twice the rate of legal publications generally."[17] For example, annual supplementation of West's *American Jurisprudence 2d* rose from $1,300.00 in 1993 to $7,106.00 in 2010, an increase of 446 percent in 17 years.[18] Lexis titles also saw huge increases from 1995–2009:

- *Moore's Federal Practice*: 46 percent

- *Bender's Federal Practice Forms*: 116 percent

- *Collier on Bankruptcy*: 140 percent

- *Nimmer on Copyright*: 167 percent[19]

What does this mean for The Big Three? An oligopoly, and a lucrative one at that. In 2010, the three publishers combined had over $12 billion in revenue.[20] Typically about 85 percent of those dollars come from supplementation—pocket parts, looseleaf pages, new volumes, and other updates.[21] Often, it costs as much to update a treatise for 1 year as to buy a new edition outright. For example, in 2008, *Fletcher Corporation Forms Annotated*, a multivolume West title, cost $2,705 to buy. The price to supplement an existing set was 8 percent higher, at $2,909. In 1993, the supplements were dirt cheap at $429, meaning the price had risen 334 percent in just 15 years.[22]

Cost-Saving Tips

What recourse do law libraries have in the face of crippling price increases? They can't get this information elsewhere, and of course they can't be without it. Law schools can raise tuition, and law firms can bill their clients more, but there are ceilings for these actions—low ceilings, in some cases. Meanwhile, prices go up, up, up. Their ceiling, it seems, is the heavens themselves.

Forced to cut costs or be shut down, librarians have come up with some effective strategies, most involving canceling print supplements for primary and secondary sources. In a treatise, for example, most of the value lies in the base text, which provides the contours of the field, its basic vocabulary, and the time-tested authorities. Supplements only pile on more cases, which you can get from Westlaw, LexisNexis, or a free website (see Chapters 5 and 6). Some libraries will buy a treatise, cancel the updates, and then buy the same treatise again in 4–5 years, saving a few thousand dollars in the process. Attorneys will still use the volumes for high-level concepts or background reading, then turn to a database to look for the latest cases, and they seem comfortable doing this.

There are exceptions, however, and if you are going to work in a law firm library, you need to identify these exceptions fast. In one large firm where I worked, the managing partner of my office, Gabriel (not his real name), was a well-known grump. He came into the library one day and asked for the *Atlantic Reporter* in print. I had thrown away a bunch of old reporters, including the *Atlantic Reporter*, because I was running out of shelf space. Moreover, the reporters had been canceled years before, and all the cases were on Westlaw and LexisNexis anyhow. I offered to pull a case for him from one of these online services, but he seemed more interested in the fate of the *Atlantic Reporter*. At that moment, I realized that its fate and mine were intertwined.

Knowing that the previous librarian had a reputation for throwing stuff out, I said maybe she had gotten rid of them. Serving up a colleague like that was not my finest professional moment, but it saved me from the noose. Gabriel looked down and shook his head. "You're probably right," he said. Then he turned and walked out of the library.

The crucial issue here is this: Law firm partners own the firm, meaning they own the library collection as well. Instead of just tossing the old reporters, I should have discussed my plan with the office administrator—the business manager who works closely with the firm management committee (see Chapter 8 for more on working with law firm management). This is the key to controlling costs in any law library: Talk to those in charge constantly. Make them experts on how much items cost and how often they are used. Ask the publishers to give you 5–10 years of supplementation costs for certain titles. You can also find this information in the outstanding *Legal Information Buyer's Guide and Reference Manual* by Kenneth Svengalis. (The book is updated annually.) Then, press your attorney users to be realistic about their usage.

Explain that certain information is available through other means—Westlaw, LexisNexis, or a cheaper but comparable treatise.

Another potential cost saver for law firms is academic or public libraries. Any library attached to a state-funded law school must be open to the public, and many of them will let attorneys check out volumes. Most private schools are also open to members of the bar. Some charge a nominal fee for library use, often a few hundred dollars a year for check-out privileges, late-night and weekend access, and on-site Westlaw and LexisNexis. Public law libraries are on the decline (see Chapter 10), but any general public library offers interlibrary loan (ILL), which I have used hundreds of times for attorney patrons. At the very least, ILL lets an attorney see a book before deciding to spend the law firm's money on it.

The last cost-saving measure is to use electronic access instead of print supplementation, especially for firms that subscribe to Westlaw or LexisNexis anyway. Why pay for the same information twice? Svengalis lists a series of West titles with an initial cost of $43,302 and a yearly update cost of $29,891. Those same titles on Westlaw cost $2,208 per year.[23] Some titles, though, are unavailable electronically or are harder to use in that format, so you need to know both services intimately, as well as the predilections of your users. For more details, see Chapters 5 and 6.

Public law libraries can also save money by canceling certain print titles and substituting electronic access. Chapter 4 discusses looseleaf services, which are prime candidates for cancellation; public libraries can also cancel legal newsletters and law journals. Most articles from the last 30 years are on Westlaw and LexisNexis, and older articles can be obtained via ILL.

Westlaw and LexisNexis can be pricey for law firms. Public libraries, however, can subscribe to cheaper, pared-down versions. With Westlaw Patron Access, for instance, access is confined to computer terminals in the library (it is not available to remote users via user passwords). Anyone who walks up to a library terminal may click the desktop link and use the database. This version also includes only the basics—case law, statutes, regulations, and the most common secondary sources. Specialized content such as public records, business sources, and news publications are not included. See Westlaw Patron Access (www.store.westlaw.com/westlaw/patron-access/default.aspx) for more information.

A similar product is LexisNexis Academic (academic.lexis nexis.com/online-services/academic/academic-overview.aspx) is intended for academic libraries. It therefore also contains news and business content, making it pricier than Westlaw Patron Access but still less expensive than the law firm version of either database.

Law Journals

Before 1879, when John West began publishing the *North Western Reporter* and other collections of cases, lawyers learned about new cases through a series of law magazines—*Albany Law Journal*, *Central Law Journal*, *American Law Review*, and *Virginia Law Journal*, to name a few. The new case reporters, however, were more current and more thorough than these magazines, and by 1900, most of the periodicals had died off. In their place rose university legal journals, or *law reviews*. Edited by students, these journals published short discussions of cases written by students, as well as longer, more scholarly works by professors, lawyers, or judges.

Which was the first law review? Lawrence Friedman, in *A History of American Law* (1973), suggests it was Harvard's, which seems to be the consensus. (Wikipedia calls *Harvard Law Review* the "oldest operating student-edited law review.") It appeared in 1887, though another journal, the *Columbia Jurist*, was actually 2 years older. According to its masthead, the *Jurist* was "published weekly by the students of the Columbia College Law School." The *Jurist* closed up shop in 1887, reappearing in 1901 as the *Columbia Law Review*. Other journals are even older, but they were published under the stewardship of nonstudents. Thus, what we can say about Harvard is that it has the oldest *continuously operating* student-edited law review in the United States.

Of course, as Harvard goes, so goes the law. Each of the 200-plus U.S. law schools now publishes its own student-edited law review, and the bigger schools publish more than one. Harvard, for instance, could fill nearly two tic-tac-toe grids with its serial excess. In addition to the main law review, the school produces the following:

- *Civil Rights-Civil Liberties Law Review*
- *Environmental Law Review*
- *Harvard Business Law Review*
- *Harvard International Law Journal*
- *Harvard Journal of the Legal Left*
- *Harvard Journal on Racial and Ethnic Justice*
- *Harvard Law and Policy Review*
- *Human Rights Journal*
- *Journal of Law and Gender*
- *Journal of Law and Public Policy*
- *Journal of Law and Technology*
- *Journal on Legislation*
- *Journal of Sports and Entertainment Law*
- *Latino Law Review*
- *National Security Journal*
- *Negotiation Law Review*

Some scholarly law journals come not from law schools but commercial publishers. Sage and Blackwell (now John Wiley & Sons) are two of the biggest, and they tend to produce interdisciplinary journals. Some examples are *Law and Literature*, *Social and Legal Studies*, and the ultraspecific *Corporate Social Responsibility and Environmental Management*. There are also newsletters, newspapers, glossy magazines, and professional journals that do exactly what those pre-West periodicals did back in the 1870s: summarize cases, discuss trends, and report on the profession (see Chapter 2).

Speaking of the profession, there is now a hot debate concerning the number and utility of law reviews. Actually, it isn't even a debate because everyone—lawyers, academics, even the bookish Supreme Court justices—agrees that law reviews tend to publish scholarship of little value to the practicing bar. Judge Richard Posner of the U.S. Seventh Circuit Court, who is also a law professor, complained in 2004 that "too many articles are too long, too dull, and too heavily annotated, and that many interdisciplinary articles are published that have no merit at all."[24] In 2008, Supreme Court Chief Justice John Roberts said, "What the academy is doing, as far as I can tell, is largely of no use or interest to people who actually practice law."[25]

Two years later, Justice Anthony Kennedy noted the decline in student-written analyses of recent cases, called *case notes*, in law reviews. In his earlier years on the Supreme Court, Kennedy had found it useful to read any law review notes discussing cases appealed to the Court. Now, there is a quicker way to meet this need: blogs. Yet case notes, Kennedy says, played an additional role, one he sees as no longer fulfilled: "It's perfectly possible and feasible, it seems to me, for law review commentary immediately to come out with reference to important three-judge district court cases, so we have some neutral, detached, critical, intellectual commentary and analysis of the case. We need that."[26]

Like Kennedy, I believe that law reviews have value. They give students some advanced research and writing training, and they provide an outlet for the kind of theorizing that would never make it into a treatise or practice guide. Before World War II, law professors and students wrote practical, profession-based articles. Since then, legal scholarship has become a "dialogue between law professors or for exchanges between the law schools and other people in the university, chiefly in the economics department, but also scholars doing research in fields such as philosophy, sociology, and political science."[27] This dialogue is important. Law is not made in a vacuum; it is a response to social and economic trends. Thus, legal scholarship is relevant, no matter what lawyers and judges say to the contrary.

Moreover, some attorneys do use law review articles. Often, the first attempt by the profession to analyze some new legal trend appears in the pages of a law review. Also, some reviews publish an annual survey of important cases in a particular area. Some academics look down on these retrospectives, seeing them as "a lower function—a pro bono service, not real, significant scholarship."[28] Plus, they point out, this service of the journals has been supplanted by newsletters, looseleafs, and electronic alerts set up through Westlaw or LexisNexis.

All of these options, however, are more expensive than the $40 annual subscription for a law review. Moreover, newsletters and alerts cite and summarize cases with no commentary, whereas the review author engages with the cases, fitting them into the legal landscape like pieces in a puzzle.

Public and Law Firm Libraries

Academic law library collections are mandated to some degree by American Bar Association accreditation standards. As a result, these collections are pretty much the same. Public and law firm libraries, however, often have very different, sometimes unique collections. A few sample collection development policies are available on the website of the Technical Services Special Interest Section of the American Association of Law Librarians (www.aall net.org/sis/tssis/committees/acquisitions/collectiondevelopment policies). Following are a few other collection development policies:

- Sacramento County, California (www.tinyurl.com/ 6woo99a)

- King County, Seattle, Washington (www.kcll.org/ contact/policies)

- Denison, Texas (www.tinyurl.com/7pw9tby)

Public law libraries have been starved for funding in recent years. Some, in fact, have died (see Chapter 10), putting the burden of legal reference service on regular public libraries, which can ill afford to add a collection of costly legal publications. Nevertheless, there are some low-cost legal materials that any public library can acquire:

- West's Nutshell series, which consists of 200 or so paperback volumes, useful to the public and practitioners alike (cost: less than $40 each)

- Rules of court for your state, available from West (cost: less than $200)

- Form books for your state, which tend to be among the cheapest titles from West and Lexis, invaluable to the public and practitioners (cost: $200–300 per title)

- *Black's Law Dictionary*, the most popular of all legal dictionaries and one of the few West titles with *no* annual updates (cost: less than $200)

- Nolo Press self-help books (cost: usually $25–40; there is nothing better for public use; see Chapter 9)

- Westlaw's or LexisNexis's steep discounts on database access to public libraries (cost: just a few hundred dollars a year for any sort of customized plan; see Chapter 5)

In my experience, most law firms do not have formal written collection management policies. One or two are available on the AALL Technical Services Special Interest Section website, and the librarian David Whelan put a sample policy on his blog back in 2002,[29] a post he updated in 2010. Thus, for guidance, you will need to rely on various books and articles about law firm collection management. Try these for starters:

- *AALL Spectrum*, the professional magazine of the American Association of Law Librarians (see Chapter 9)[30]

- Chapter 23 of Svengalis's *Legal Information Buyer's Guide and Reference Manual*

- Law Librarian Blog (www.lawprofessors.typepad.com/law_librarian_blog)

- Strategic Librarian (www.strategiclibrarian.com), whose tag line is "Using Strategy to develop the law firm library"

Endnotes

1. Stephen Elias and Susan Levinkind, *Legal Research: How to Find and Understand the Law,* 11th ed. (Berkeley, CA: Nolo, 2003), 3/2.
2. For a thorough discussion of American common law, see Lawrence M. Friedman, *A History of American Law* (New York: Simon & Schuster, 1985).
3. Ever wonder why mattress tags are there in the first place? See Mary Whisner, "Mattress Tags and Pillow Cases," *Law Library Journal* 101, no. 2 (2009): 235–247. The article illustrates a good example of the relationship between regulations and statutes.
4. Two other primary sources are treaties and city or county ordinances. A great introduction to treaties is the Georgetown Law Library Treaty Research Guide (www.ll.georgetown.edu/guides/

TreatyResearch.cfm). For ordinances, a good introduction is Researching Local Government Law (lawweb.usc.edu/library/research/uslaw/multilaw/municipal.cfm).

5.   David J. Seip, introduction to *Statham's Abridgement of the Law*, trans. Margaret Klingelsmith (Clark, NJ: Lawbook Exchange, Ltd., 2007), xiii.

6.   Kendall Svengalis, *Legal Information Buyer's Guide and Reference Manual* (Barrington, RI: Rhode Island Press, 2011), 8.

7.   Ibid.

8.   Erin Carlyle, "Westlaw Rises to Legal Publishing Fame by Selling Free Information," Citypages, April 29, 2009, accessed November 19, 2012, www.citypages.com/2009-04-29/news/westlaw-rises-to-legal-publishing-fame-by-selling-free-information.

9.   Robert M. Jarvis, "John B. West: Founder of the West Publishing Company," *American Journal of Legal History* 50, no. 1 (2010): 5.

10.   Ibid., 6.

11.   Ibid., 8.

12.   The publisher founded by John B. West has had multiple names. It is currently a subsidiary of Thomson Reuters. In this book, I will refer to the print publisher simply as *West*; the company's electronic database will be referred to as *Westlaw*. Likewise, I will refer to the publisher LexisNexis simply as *Lexis*; the company's electronic database will be referred to as *LexisNexis*. See Chapter 5 for more information on Westlaw and LexisNexis.

13.   Svengalis, *Legal Information Buyer's Guide*, 12.

14.   Amanda Runyon, "The Effect of Economics and Electronic Resources on the Traditional Law Library Print Collection," *Law Library Journal* 101, no. 2 (2009): 177–205.

15.   In 2008, after a merger with the U.K.-based Reuters Group, Thomson West became Thomson Reuters. Headquartered in New York, it is still principally owned by the Canadian Thomson Corporation, preserving the irony of most of American law being published by non-U.S. companies.

16.   Gary P. Rodrigues, "More Speculation on Mergers and Acquisitions in Legal Publishing," Slaw (online legal magazine), December 13, 2010, accessed November 19, 2012, www.slaw.ca/2010/12/13/acquisitions-and-mergers-in-legal-publishing-not-over.

17.   Runyon, "Effect of Economics," 180.

18.   Kendall F. Svengalis, *Legal Information Buyer's Guide and Reference Manual* (Barrington, RI: Rhode Island Press, 2011), 42.

19. Emory School of Law, "Price Increases," accessed November 19, 2012, library.law.emory.edu/for-law-students/emory-law-subject-guides/the-legal-research-industry/price-increases.

20. Emory School of Law, "Mergers and Acquisitions," accessed November 19, 2012, library.law.emory.edu/for-law-students/emory-law-subject-guides/the-legal-research-industry/mergers-and-acquisitions.

21. Emory School of Law, "Price Increases."

22. Kendall Svengalis, "Legal Information: Globalization, Conglomerates and Competition—Monopoly or Free Market," PowerPoint slides, May 19, 2009, www.rilawpress.com.

23. Ibid.

24. Richard A. Posner, "Against the Law Reviews," *Legal Affairs* (November/December 2004), accessed November 19, 2012, www.legalaffairs.org/issues/November-December-2004/review_posner_novdec04.msp.

25. Adam Liptak, "Keep the Briefs Brief, Literary Justices Advise," *New York Times*, May 20, 2011, accessed November 19, 2012, www.tinyurl.com/89xfuyj.

26. Richard A. Danner, Kelly Leong, and Wayne V. Miller, "The Durham Statement Two Years Later: Open Access in the Law School Journal Environment," *Law Library Journal* 103, no. 1 (2011): 39–54.

27. Richard Harnsberger, "Reflections about Law Reviews and American Legal Scholarship," *Nebraska Law Review* 76 (1997): 693.

28. James Milles, "Redefining Open Access for the Legal Information Market," *Law Library Journal* 98, no. 4 (2006): 633.

29. David Whelan, "Sample Collection Development Policy," David Whelan: Explorations with Information and Technology (blog), April 30, 2002, accessed November 19, 2012, www.ofaolain.com/blog/2002/04/30/sample-collection-development-policy.

30. An illustrative article is Steve Lastres, "Collection Development in the Age of the Virtual Law Firm Library," *AALL Spectrum*, June 2011, 20–23.

Chapter 2

The Kolor-Koded, Turnkey-Shaped Streamline Basics of Legal Research

"Boy, it's been slow," remarked Blaydon Graycastle,[1] a New Jersey criminal defense attorney, walking out of his office to stand by his paralegal's desk. "We haven't had a client all day." Blaydon's paralegal, Amanda, nodded in agreement. She made the winning click in her 10th straight game of computer Solitaire and stifled a yawn.

As the digital cards flitted across the screen, the front door opened, and a woman walked in out of the rain. She was tall and slender, and though her long blonde hair was soaked, it fell lusciously over her shoulders. She opened her overcoat to reveal a form-fitting black dress, and Amanda caught a whiff of Victoria's Secret perfume. Letting her overcoat slide to the floor, the blonde walked over to Blaydon. She sat on the corner of Amanda's desk, her hair dripping on the calendar.

"Mr. Graycastle," the blonde said huskily, "I need your help. My darling Uncle Howard died last year. In fact, he killed himself. He left his whole estate"—her shoulders rose and fell on the word *whole*—"to me. But now my Aunt Bloddie is saying Uncle Howard's will is no good. She said he was crazy. I said he wasn't, and she said, 'Well, he had to be if he killed himself, right?' So she hasn't let me have one single *dime*."

Pulling a handkerchief from her handbag, the blonde dabbed her cornflower blue eyes. Amanda rolled her own hazel ones, stood up from her chair, and excused herself. Blaydon blinked, then ran a hand through his salt-and-syrup (not quite dark enough to be pepper) hair. Finally, he found his composure. "So what you need to know, miss," he said, "is whether suicide is evidence of insanity for the purpose of challenging a will in New Jersey. Is that it?"

Rising from the desk, the blonde moved close enough to Blaydon Graycastle to read the tag on his shirt. Her smile revealed a set of teeth like a drawer of gleaming knives. "That's it ex-*actly*," she said, putting her arms around Blaydon and hugging him like a brother just returned from war. Amanda walked into the office, saw the spectacle, and walked right back out.

The Librarian's Role

While most legal inquiries are generally somewhat less dramatic, what is the librarian's role in such a scenario? Blaydon, the attorney, is responsible for advising the client, designing her legal strategy, and, if necessary, representing her in court. Amanda, the paralegal, can draft documents, organize the case files, and assist in trial preparation. As the librarian (of course, a solo practitioner would not employ a librarian, but play along here), I might be asked to find New Jersey statutes on wills. Or suss out any relevant case law. Or come up with a form challenging the estate. In other words, I would have to help with the *research*.

There are many books that can teach you the process of legal research, some of which are discussed in Chapter 9. For now, I want to give you the basics.

Statutes

Recall from Chapter 1 that statutes are a primary source, meaning they are "the law." Statutes are published in several formats: session laws, statutory codes, and annotated codes. *Session laws* are the collection of bills passed by the legislature during its annual session. These laws are printed in chronological order with no regard to subject. Thus, a bankruptcy law amendment could be placed between one on Social Security and one reorganizing the Department of the Interior. The session laws publication contains the official text of the law as passed by the legislature. U.S. session laws, for example, are compiled in a series called *Statutes at Large.*

After first appearing in the session laws, statutes are then reprinted in a *statutory code,* a subject arrangement of current laws. The U.S. Code organizes all federal statutes into 50 subject areas called *titles.* Each title is subdivided into numbered sections. State statutes have similar organizations, though they may use different terms. In North Carolina, for example, the subject groups are called *chapters* instead of *titles.*

An *annotated code* includes more than the statutes. It also includes notes on the history of each statute (i.e., when it was enacted and later amended), cases that interpret the statute, regulations authorized by the statute, and references to journal articles, treatises, and other sources on the same subject. These notes are called *annotations,* and they are meant to help the researcher by directing her to other relevant material. There are two annotated versions of the U.S. Code, one published by West (*United States Code Annotated*) and the other published by Lexis (*United States Code Service*). These are considered unofficial codes—the official one is published by the U.S.—but most researchers prefer to use them because of the annotations, since the official code has none. No state publishes its own code; that duty is left to West and/ or Lexis.

Statutory codes are updated with new laws in two ways. First, softbound supplements are issued quarterly containing the changes made to each code section. These supplements sit on the library shelf at the end of the code set. Each year, those pamphlets are replaced by pocket parts, which are saddle-stapled pamphlets with a thick card stapled or glued to one cover. Each pocket part contains that year's changes to its corresponding volume. The card is inserted into a pocket in the back of the volume, thereby updating the volume for that year. Many hardbound treatises and practice guides are also updated by annual pocket parts.

Statutes can be identified by citation, subject, or popular name. A *citation* is a reference to a legal precedent or authority, such as a case, statute, or treatise. U.S. statute citations consist of the title number, the abbreviated code name, and the section number. Thus, 42 USC § 1983 means:

Title	Name of Code	Section (§)
42	USC (United States Code)	1983

State statutes vary in their citation formats, which can be somewhat confusing until you get the hang of them. Some examples are:

- Iowa Code § 259A.1
- N.C. Gen. Stat. § 25-1-101
- Ohio Rev. Code § 1301.01
- 13 Pa. Cons. Stat. § 1101
- Tex. Bus. & Com. Code § 1.101

The definitive guide to these formats—to *all* legal citations, in fact—is *The Bluebook: A Uniform System of Citation*, commonly called *The Bluebook*. Many legal reference questions pertain to the intricacies and oddities of legal citation, so study *The Bluebook*. Master it. Be able to find things in it quickly.

If you don't have a citation, then you may be able to find a statute by *subject*. Session laws are not organized by subject, but the statutory codes are. Each code also has a multivolume index covering the entire code. Always look up your topic in the index first. Why? The topic is probably addressed in more than one statute. The index will cross-reference all the statutes relevant to a particular topic.

You may also be asked to find a statute by its *popular name*, such as the Endangered Species Act, the Clean Air Act, or the No Child Left Behind Act. Usually, this name appears in the statute itself, though some names, like Megan's Law, are informal, unofficial monikers. Each code set has a Popular Name Table, a separate pamphlet listing these names in alphabetical order along with the citations to the statutes.

Cases

Cases are another primary source. Recall from Chapter 1 that cases, also called *opinions*, are collected in print sets called *reporters*. West publishes the most important, but not all, opinions from the 50 states and the District of Columbia in seven regional reporters: Atlantic, North Eastern, North Western, Pacific, South Eastern, South Western, and Southern. It publishes United States federal court cases in the *Federal Reporter* (appellate), *Federal Supplement* (trial), and *Supreme Court Reporter*. There is also a line of West specialty reporters such as the *Bankruptcy Reporter*, *Military Justice Reporter*, *Veterans Appeals Reporter*, *American Tribal Law Reporter*, *Federal Rules Decisions*, *Education Law Reporter*, and *Federal Claims Reporter*. Together, these reporters make up the *National Reporter System*.[2]

In addition to printing the cases, West staff members add a number of editorial features to help researchers. These include the synopsis, headnotes, and topics/key numbers.

Synopsis

The synopsis is simply a brief description that includes the facts of the case, the holding of the court, the lower court's decision in the case, and the name of the judge writing the opinion.

Headnotes

Opinions always involve at least one legal issue, or point of law. West editors identify the legal issues in each case and summarize those issues in one-sentence *headnotes*, which are printed at the top of the case like a table of contents. Headnotes are numbered, and each is followed by a topic name and key number like this: Criminal Law ☛ 731.

Topics/Key Numbers

All of American law is broken down into more than 400 broad topics. (West started with just 200 in the 1800s.) Each of these is divided into narrower topics, which are in turn divided into even narrower topics, like steps in an outline. There can be up to eight steps in the hierarchy until you reach an individual point of law. Each point of law has a unique number called a *key number*. Each headnote is paired with a topic and key number, and that topic/key number pair represents *only that* point of law. Thus, wherever you see that topic/key number pair, you know that the point of law it represents appears in that opinion.

Advance Sheets

Case reporters are tan hardbound volumes with black and red stripes. As cases are decided, however, West first prints them in softbound pamphlets called *advance sheets*. These can be printed and shipped faster than bound reporters, meaning the libraries get new cases within a week or so of their resolution. West later sends a bound reporter to replace the latest four or five advance sheets, which can then be discarded.

Some other series, such as *American Law Reports*, also use the advance sheets method, as do cases published directly by state governments. The *United States Reports* (published by the federal government) does not use advance sheets.

Digests

Case reporters don't have subject indexes. A case can be located by subject using one of West's many *digests*, which are series of books that arrange headnotes alphanumerically by topic and key number. Headnotes from different cases that discuss the same point of law appear together in a digest, and the same headnote may appear in two or more places in the digest. Moreover, the key numbers assigned to points of law are uniform throughout all the digests. So, for example, when you find a relevant case in the *Washington Digest*, you can look under the same topic and key number in the *North Carolina Digest* and find other relevant cases.

Case Citations

Case citations consist of the reporter volume number, abbreviated name, and beginning page number of the case. Thus, 238 F.3d 68 means:

Vol. No.	Reporter	Page No.
238	F.3d (*Federal Reporter*, 3rd series)	68

State case citations can be tricky, especially since some states publish their own reporters independent of the West reporter (see Chapter 1). Thus, you could have two different citations to the same case.

For example, *Nolan v. Village of Martin*, a 2006 case in North Carolina, can be cited either as 360 N.C. 256 (*North Carolina Reports*, published by the state) or 624 S.E.2d 305 (*South Eastern Reporter*, 2nd series, published by West). U.S. Supreme Court cases are even trickier, as they have three citations to deal with. Thus, the 1988 case *Shapero v. Kentucky Bar Association* can appear as 486 U.S. 466 (*U.S. Reports*, published by the federal government) or 108 S.Ct. 1916 (*Supreme Court Reporter*, published by West) or 100 L.Ed.2d 475 (*Supreme Court Reports*, Lawyer's Edition, published by LexisNexis). As with statutes, your best guide to decoding case citation formats is *The Bluebook*.

To find a case by subject, you will need one of the West digests. (Remember: The case reporters do not have indexes.) Digests print summaries of cases and arrange them alphabetically by topic, then numerically by key number. There is at least one digest corresponding to each West reporter. So, for example, to find a Georgia case on a criminal law topic, you would

1. Determine an appropriate topic and key number. (Start with the Descriptive Word Index, the two or three volumes at the end of the digest that connect everyday terms to the topic and key number system.)

2. Look up that topic and key number in the *West Georgia Digest* (or in the *South Eastern Digest*, which also covers North Carolina, South Carolina, Virginia, and West Virginia).

3. Read the case summaries under that key number until you find a suitable one.

4. Look up the case by the citation given in the digest.

Each digest also has a name table, listing all the cases it covers by plaintiff and defendant. This is useful for requests such as "I need that West Virginia case—gosh, it was a few years back—where the town of Charleston got sued." That could be any of a number of cases, but you could find them all by looking up *Charleston* as a defendant in the name table in the *South Eastern Digest*.

Shepard's and KeyCite

After finding cases on point, you will need to verify that they are still "good law"—that they have not been criticized or overturned by subsequent cases. (A case that is no longer "good law" should not be cited in a legal memo or brief.) You do this by looking up your case in a *citator*, which lists all the authorities, primary and secondary, that cite your case. The listing also indicates how your case is regarded.

For decades, the leading citator was *Shepard's Citations*, begun by Frank Shepard in 1873. LexisNexis acquired it in 1996, creating an online version in 1999, 2 years after West had introduced its electronic citator, KeyCite. Both services use color-coded systems of icons to indicate how cases have been treated by subsequent authorities, a process that is often called "Shepardizing." (It is called this even when KeyCite is used.) See Figure 2.1 for the *Shepard's* and KeyCite symbols. For more about *Shepard's* and KeyCite, see Chapter 5.

Administrative Law

A third area of primary law is administrative law, a major source of which is the regulations, or *regs*, created by a federal or state agency. Regs have the same authority as statutes, but they are far more numerous and detailed. Federal regulations must be published first in proposed form and again in final form. They initially appear in the *Federal Register*, a daily journal of agency activities.

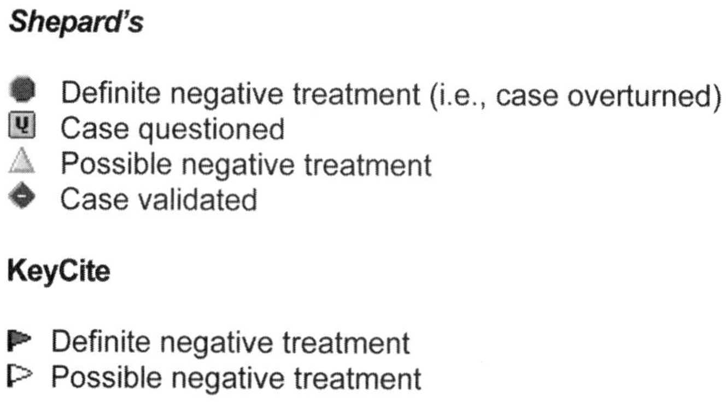

Shepard's

● Definite negative treatment (i.e., case overturned)
Ⓤ Case questioned
△ Possible negative treatment
◆ Case validated

KeyCite

▶ Definite negative treatment
▷ Possible negative treatment

Figure 2.1   *Shepard's* and KeyCite symbols

The public has the opportunity to comment on proposed regs by writing to the agency or visiting www.regulations.gov.

After the comment period, the agency may rewrite the regs and resubmit them for additional comments. Eventually, they will be published in final form in the *Code of Federal Regulations* (*CFR*). The *CFR* is organized into 50 titles—the same titles, in fact, as the U.S. Code—which are divided into parts, then into sections. The states have a similar publication system for their regulations.

In addition to their rulemaking powers, federal and state agencies can issue guidance documents, policy statements, and rulings on certain types of cases. These rulings are generally as binding and authoritative as court decisions. For example, the North Carolina Utilities Commission has "full power to administer oaths and to hear and take evidence" in utilities disputes, and it "renders decisions upon questions of law and fact in the same manner as a court of record."[3] It is sometimes hard to find these types of documents, especially for state agencies. One excellent source is State and Local Government on the Net (www.statelocalgov.net).

A final source of administrative law is executive orders. A presidential executive order "is a directive issued to federal agencies, department heads, or other federal employees by the President of the United States under his statutory or constitutional powers."[4] These orders do not require congressional approval, but they do have the legal authority of statutes. A good source for these and other presidential documents—speeches, proclamations, reports, and more—is the American Presidency Project (www.presidency. ucsb.edu). State governors also issue executive orders that are binding within their states.[5]

Secondary Sources

As explained in Chapter 1, primary sources—statutes, cases, agency regs and rulings, executive orders, treaties, and local ordinances—

are "the law." The previous sections have discussed some methods for locating these documents by citation or topic. Often, however, researchers begin with a *secondary source*, a publication that explains, summarizes, or helps locate the law. Attorneys often refer to these publications using abbreviations or just the author's last name (e.g., Wright and Miller, *Bluebook, CJS, Robinson*, or *WFPD*).[6] There are several categories of secondary sources.

Digests

As previously discussed, West digests are used to find cases published in the *National Reporter System*. Each regional reporter has a corresponding digest, and the *West Federal Practice Digest* covers the *Federal Reporter, Federal Supplement*, and *Supreme Court Reporter*. There are also some specialty digests such as the *West Bankruptcy Digest*.

Encyclopedias

A legal encyclopedia provides introductory articles on all areas of American law, citing major cases and statutes for each area. The two national encyclopedias are *American Jurisprudence* and *Corpus Juris Secundum*, both published by West.[7] In addition, West publishes legal encyclopedias for many states, for example *South Carolina Jurisprudence, Illinois Law and Practice*, and *Strong's North Carolina Index*.

A legal encyclopedia doesn't work like a regular encyclopedia. If you want an overview of, say, giraffes, just grab the G volume of *World Book* or *Grolier's* and look up *giraffes* to find all the information in one spot. But a single article can't discuss all aspects of a legal topic. As an example, let's consider tax. A legal encyclopedia would have a general article on tax, but other subjects also have tax implications: bankruptcy, finance, real estate sales, corporate mergers, and employee benefits, to name a few. Those implications are mentioned in the general tax article, but their fullest discussion occurs in the articles for those other subjects.[8]

American Law Reports

Published since 1919, *American Law Reports* (*ALR*) is a hybrid of primary and secondary sources. Each bound volume reprints several important cases, but since cases are also available in reporters, these are not the purpose of *ALR*. Also appearing with each case is an in-depth article written by a legal expert on the subject of that case. These articles are called *annotations*. (You may recall that the citations to cases, journal articles, and other sources printed with the statutes in an annotated code are also called annotations. Don't be confused by this—it's the same word, but with a different context and meaning.)

ALR annotations are similar to articles in legal encyclopedias. Both are wide-ranging and comprehensive, and both include abundant citations to statutes, cases, and other secondary sources on the same topic. However, *ALR* annotations are published chronologically like case reporters, not alphabetically like encyclopedia articles, and they tend to delve more deeply into a specific legal principle or doctrine. In addition, *ALR* annotations discuss cases on both sides of the legal issue, making them better sources for preparing arguments.

ALR is currently in its sixth series (it is abbreviated as *ALR*6th). Earlier series are referred to as *ALR*, *ALR*2d, and so on. Since these annotations can deal with state or federal issues, a separate federal-only series, *ALR Fed*, was introduced in the 1990s. (It is now in its second series, *ALR Fed* 2d.) A combined *ALR Index* covers *ALR*2d–*ALR*6th and both federal series. There is also an *ALR Digest*, which organizes annotations based on the West topic and key number system.

Restatements of the Law

The *Restatements of the Law* are a longstanding, highly respected set of treatises on various broad subjects. Begun in 1923, there are now three series of *Restatements*, all jointly published by West and the American Law Institute, an organization of legal academics and practitioners. Though not binding authority, *Restatements* are very persuasive and are often cited by judges in opinions (over 150,000 citations, according to one estimate). As explained on the Harvard Law School Library website, the aim of the *Restatements* is to "distill the 'black letter law' from cases, to indicate a trend in common law, and, occasionally, to recommend what a rule of law should be. In essence, they restate existing common law into a series of principles or rules."[9]

Each Restatement section begins with a "black letter" principle, written like a statute but not passed by a legislature. In other words, the principle itself has no force of law; it is a truth derived from close readings of numerous cases. Following this principle are the sections Comments, Illustrations, and Reporters' Notes, which is a detailed discussion of the cases that goes into the black-letter principle. *Restatements* are still being written (see the American Law Institute website at www.ali.org for drafts of the in-progress *Restatement of Employment Law*) and new cases are being added to the notes of existing *Restatements*.

Treatises

Treatises are multivolume works, similar to encyclopedias, but with two key differences: Treatises are more in-depth, and they are dedicated to a single topic. Legal treatises "represent a lifetime of scholarly investigation and writing, reflecting the unified perspective of an influential legal scholar."[10] Many titles follow the same pattern: [original author's name] on [subject]. Examples include:

- *Wigmore on Evidence*

- *Nimmer on Copyright*

- *Corbin on Contracts*

- *Powell on Real Property*

Some treatises are hardbound books updated by pocket parts. Others have looseleaf pages contained in a three-ring binder or a post-hole binder. These are updated by replacing existing pages with new ones. The Georgetown Law Library maintains a webpage describing the leading treatises in 50 subject areas (www.law. georgetown.edu/library/research/treatise-finders/index.cfm).

Practice Guides

Practice guides are not, in the strictest sense, treatises, though they are often called such. Instead, they are shorter (1–2 volumes) and less in-depth, and they have features lacking in the true treatise— forms, examples, case studies, checklists, and bibliographies, to name a few. Practice guides, as the name implies, are written to satisfy the day-to-day needs of the working attorney. So while a treatise might describe the elements of a legal claim, for example, a practice guide might assist in drafting a complaint based on that claim or drafting a contract that avoids raising that claim. Examples include:

- Michael Jordan, *Drafting Wills and Trust Agreements*, 4th edition

- Ruggero J. Aldisert, *Winning on Appeal: Better Briefs and Oral Argument*, 2nd edition

- Thomas A. Mauet, *Trial Techniques*, 8th edition

- Alan Kaminsky and Karen L. Campbell, *The Lawyer's Guide to Lead Paint, Asbestos, and Chinese Drywall*

Form Books

Despite the popular media image of attorneys as courtroom orators, most attorneys write for a living. Complaints, answers, agreements, amendments, briefs, motions, licenses, contracts, wills, and disclaimers are all documents that attorneys are expected to wordsmith. Rarely do they have to draft anything original. Instead, they modify forms found in titles such as:

- *West's Legal Forms*
- *American Jurisprudence Pleading and Practice Forms*
- *Thorp's North Carolina Trial Practice Forms*
- *New Jersey Law With Forms*

These forms are actually templates. A complaint in *West's Legal Forms*, for example, is a document shell with standard legal language. An attorney would adapt this template by adding the facts of her client's case, the causes of action (i.e., reasons for suing), and the client's demand.

Serials

Chapter 1 discussed law reviews and scholarly law journals. There are indexes to locating articles from these journals. *Index to Legal Periodicals* covers articles from the early 1900s to 1980, while its successor, *Current Legal Index*, begins with 1980. Most researchers, however, retrieve articles electronically. Westlaw and Lexis are the biggest sources (see Chapter 5), though their coverage dates only from the 1980s. Older articles, some dating back to the 1800s, are available on HeinOnline (see Chapter 6). ProQuest and J-STOR also have full-text articles. In addition, LegalTrac (see Chapter 6), a subset of the Gale database InfoTrac, indexes more than 1,500 law reviews.

Westlaw, Lexis, and LegalTrac also cover hundreds of nonscholarly legal serials. There are several types.

Newspapers

Legal newspapers look and read like regular newspapers, except they are limited to legal practice. Chapter 1 mentioned the Dolan Company (www.thedolancompany.com), which publishes numerous state-specific papers. Another leading paper is the *National Law Journal*, published by ALM (www.law.com). ALM[11] has a few specialty newspapers as well, namely *Corporate Counsel*, which caters to in-house company attorneys, and *Law Technology News*.

Dolan and ALM also publish state-specific newspapers. The states Dolan covers include North Carolina, South Carolina, Virginia, Massachusetts, Michigan, Missouri, and Rhode Island. (I remember when only two or three states were covered.) ALM picks up Georgia, Pennsylvania, New Jersey, New York, Texas, Delaware, Connecticut, and a few more. The state papers are a fantastic source of case summaries (for cases that don't make a law review or treatise), news on prominent attorneys and law firms in that state, and substantive but not scholarly articles on matters of state law, which are not always discussed in law reviews and treatises.

Magazines

Law magazines are glossy, well-reported, national periodicals (think *Newsweek* for the field of law). The most well-known is *American Lawyer*, ALM's flagship periodical (it's the source of the A and L in the company's name). Blogs are slowly replacing the typical news article, but *American Lawyer* offers in-depth coverage and feature writing, for which blogs are an inadequate substitute. In addition, every year *American Lawyer* releases the AmLaw 100, a ranking of the country's largest and most lucrative law firms. Other rankings published in *American Lawyer* include:

- Dealmakers of the Year

- Pro Bono Scorecard

- Litigation Department of the Year

- Summer Associates Survey

The other major publisher of glossy law magazines is the American Bar Association (www.americanbar.org). Its main title is

ABA Journal, "read by more than half of the nation's 1.1 million lawyers."[12] Other titles are specific to certain practitioners (e.g., *Judges' Journal, SciTech Lawyer,* and *Student Lawyer*) or practice areas (e.g., *Antitrust, Litigation,* and *Probate & Property*).

Bar Association Periodicals

To practice law in a particular state, you must be a member of that state's bar. One of the perks of bar membership is a subscription to that bar association's professional periodical. Unlike the afore-mentioned legal newsletters and magazines, bar journals publish articles written by amateur journalists: members of the bar. Still, some are substantive, often more so than in the newspapers. In fact, they can approach law review articles, with footnotes and other hallmarks of scholarly writing. And, of course, state bar journals include news blurbs about the states' lawyers and law firms.

Some city or county bar associations also publish their own newspapers or newsletters. These tend to be like family newsletters, highlighting good deeds, retirements, chapter meetings, upcoming events, and the like. The articles deal not with substantive law but with professional concerns—avoiding malpractice claims, for example, or picking the right office billing software.

Newsletters

The biggest category of secondary sources is newsletters. See Chapter 4 for more in-depth information on newsletters.

Looseleaf Publications

Looseleaf publications are a special category of secondary sources and will be covered in Chapter 4.

Tips for Finding Information in Legal Serials

- Some serials are only on Westlaw, some only on Lexis, and many are on neither, nor are they anywhere else online (no matter what attorneys want to believe).

- You can find citations to articles about specific cases or statutes by Shepardizing or KeyCiting the case (see Chapter 5).

- Treatises, practice guides, and other secondary sources also provide citations to relevant law review articles. Occasionally they reference nonscholarly articles as well.

- For more information on legal serials, see Chapters 20 and 21 of Svengalis, *Legal Information Buyer's Guide.*

Directories

There are plenty of websites that contain online lawyer directories. For some, the directory is the primary focus. For others, it is secondary to legal guides, articles, do-it-yourself forms, and other content. In 2011, blogger Robert Ambrogi ranked the top 12 online directories using a database of website statistics.[13]

There is one directory, however, that has always been the gold standard: *Martindale-Hubbell Law Directory* (www.martindale.com). First published in 1868 as *The Martindale Directory*, its original purpose was to furnish "the address of one reliable law firm, one reliable bank, and one reliable real estate office in every city in the United States."[14] Later, the directory expanded to include lawyer ratings and listings of international firms, and in 1930, Martindale bought the rights to *Hubbell's Legal Directory*, adding that publication's digest of the collected laws of each state.[15]

Those digests, which came to include non-U.S. jurisdictions, are a key feature of *Martindale-Hubbell*, as most attorneys call it.

They make a handy reference and do *not* appear at www.martin dale.com, which may explain why many law firms buy the print set every year. These annual purchases are likely to change, however, as LexisNexis, which has owned *Martindale-Hubbell* since the 1990s, stopped updating the U.S. law digests in 2010. The foreign digest was expected in 2011, but it was not published.[16]

What should libraries do with previous years' volumes? Some keep the volume for their state because, from time to time, some-one will need to know whether Attorney So-and-So was licensed in that state in 1988 (and looking in *Martindale-Hubbell* is quicker than calling the State Bar). I have given other volumes to office decorators, amateur and professional, who like the stately look of the *Martindale-Hubbell* binding.

Citing Secondary Sources

Secondary sources are a great place to get background information and citations to cases, statutes, and other primary sources. Generally, they are not to be cited as authority in a legal memo or brief, although some secondary sources are so well-respected that judges consider them *persuasive authority*. Unlike *mandatory authority*, which judges have to follow when making their rulings, persuasive authority is only that—persuasive, although judges often follow it, especially when there is no mandatory authority directly on the topic.

Treatises, depending on the prestige of the author, may be cited as persuasive authority. Some are even cited by judges in their written opinions. Since 2001, for example, *Prosser and Keeton on the Law of Torts* has been cited more than 1,100 times by federal judges alone (I determined this by searching LexisNexis for *prosser /2 keeton* for the previous 10 years). Other oft-cited sources are:

- *Restatements of the Law*

- Laurence Tribe, *American Constitutional Law*

- Charles Alan Wright et. al., *Federal Practice and Procedure*
- *Weinstein's Evidence*
- *Collier on Bankruptcy*

A law review article, too, may be considered persuasive authority, depending on its quality, the author's credentials, and the journal's reputation. (Comments or case notes written by students are unlikely to be persuasive.) According to a 2008 ranking,[17] the top 10 law reviews are:

1. *Harvard Law Review*
2. *Yale Law Journal*
3. *Columbia Law Review*
4. *California Law Review*
5. *University of Pennsylvania Law Review*
6. *New York University Law Review*
7. *Stanford Law Review*
8. *Virginia Law Review*
9. *Cornell Law Review*
10. *UCLA Law Review*

Blaydon Graycastle: Reprise

So how would Blaydon Graycastle research the issues raised by his curvaceous client? One option is to start with a secondary source. This is often the recommended approach, especially in an unfamiliar area of law, because secondary sources can help focus your research. I would not recommend this approach for Blaydon's issue, however. Wills are governed by state law, so a national encyclopedia (e.g., *American Jurisprudence*) or general treatise (e.g.,

Williston on Wills) would be too broad. A state encyclopedia might work, but New Jersey doesn't have one.

When a good secondary source isn't available, then annotated statutes are a good place to start. There is not a relevant statute for every legal issue, but if one exists for this topic, Blaydon needs to know about it. Plus, with annotated statutes, he can find related cases listed in the statute volume. Start with the index to the *New Jersey Statutes Annotated.* Look up *wills.* A subheading for *competency* leads to N.J. Stat. Ann. § 3B:3-1, which states: "Any individual 18 or more years of age who is of sound mind may make a will and may appoint a testamentary guardian."

So what does "sound mind" mean? To most people, suicide is attempted only by someone with a mental problem. But is a mental problem the equivalent of an *un*sound mind? The statute isn't clear on this question, which is the bugbear with statutes: They can't anticipate every situation. This is one reason cases are tried and opinions are written—to interpret vague or unhelpful statutes. Maybe the annotations list a case interpreting this statute in light of suicide attempts. If not, then Blaydon can go directly to the case law.

To locate the case law, turn to one of the West digests. In this scenario, Blaydon would want the *Atlantic Digest,* which includes New Jersey. Using the digest, he would find the following combination of headnote, topic, and key number:

Wills ⚷— 55(8) – Suicide by testator

Suicide does not of itself indicate insanity and does not permit any presumption of a fixed or lasting mental aberration.

The case is *In re Rein's Will,* 50 A.2d 380 (1946). Locating the actual case in the *Atlantic Reporter,* Blaydon would find this passage:

> [S]uicide or attempted suicide is not in and of itself
> · proof of mental incapacity to make a will or proof of
> general insanity. It cannot be presumed. Suicide is very

frequently the act of a person deprived of all reason and self-restraint. But often, it is the recourse of those who ponder over their particular problem and bring to that problem all their faculties and powers of reasoning, reaching the bitter conclusion that to them life is not worth such ordeal as they suffer. Too many persons have not the consolation of religion or the arresting influence of some other sustaining philosophy to make them able "to bear the ills we have than fly to others we know not of."

Good news, then, for Blaydon's client: Her aunt can't claim that Uncle Howard was crazy just because he killed himself. Blaydon told her this in his office a few days later, when she stopped in wearing a black turtleneck, tight leopard-print pants, and lipstick the color of barroom smoke. She threw her arms around the lawyer, *her* lawyer, and kissed his lips. In the distance, Blaydon heard church bells, the clink of forks on fine china, and his brother giving a best-man toast. Amanda, doing one of the thousand thankless tasks that fall to paralegals, walked over to the couple, put her face next to Blaydon's other cheek, and said, "Excuse me, Mr. Graycastle. Your wife is on line 1."

Endnotes

1. Unlike Gabriel, the grumpy law firm managing partner, Blaydon Graycastle is a total figment of my imagination.
2. For an interactive map of the *National Reporter System*, see www.law school.westlaw.com/userguides/nationalreporter/west_map_reg_v5. html.
3. "History and Description," North Carolina Utilities Commission, accessed November 19, 2012, www.ncuc.commerce.state.nc.us/ overview/ucdesc.htm.

4. Robert Longley, "Presidential Executive Orders," About.com, accessed November 19, 2012, www.usgovinfo.about.com/od/the presidentandcabinet/a/Presidential-Executive-Orders.htm.

5. For more detailed coverage of administrative law, see the Gallagher Law Library's research guide at lib.law.washington.edu/content/ guides/adminus. For discussion of researching specific regulatory areas—tax, securities, banking, immigration, and more—see Penny A. Hazelton, *Specialized Legal Research* (Aspen Publishers).

6. These are, respectively, *Federal Practice and Procedure* (original authors: Charles Alan Wright and Arthur Miller); *The Bluebook: A Uniform System of Citation*; *Corpus Juris Secundum*; *Robinson's North Carolina Corporation Law*; and *West's Federal Practice Digest*.

7. *American Jurisprudence* was once published by Lawyers Cooperative Publishing, a competitor to West and its *Corpus Juris Secundum*. Thomson acquired both companies in the 1990s and continues to publish both titles as West products.

8. See "2011 Legal Encyclopedias Tutorial," YouTube video, 10:11, posted by "burgerlibrary," August 25, 2011, www.youtube.com/ watch?v=pH_cD3RTv3M.

9. "Secondary Sources: ALRs, Encyclopedias, Law Reviews, Restatements, & Treatises," Harvard Law School Library, February 16, 2011, accessed April 3, 2013, libguides.law.harvard.edu/content. php?pid=103327&sid=1036651.

10. Kendall Svengalis, *Legal Information Buyer's Guide and Reference Manual* (Barrington, RI: Rhode Island Law Press, 1996), 147.

11. Formerly known as American Lawyer Media, the company has rebranded itself alphabetically much like BP (once British Petroleum), NBC (an erstwhile National Broadcasting Company), and ESPN (who knew that stood for Eastern Sports Program Network?).

12. "American Bar Association Journal," American Bar Association, accessed November 19, 2012, www.tinyurl.com/cu3rybz.

13. Robert J. Ambrogi, "Popular Legal Directories, Ranked by Traffic," LawSites, June 8, 2011, accessed April 3, 2013, www.lawsitesblog. com/2011/06/popular-legal-directories-ranked-by-traffic.html.

14. "About Martindale-Hubbell," martindale.com, accessed November 19, 2012, www.martindale.com/About_Martindale-Hubbell/index. aspx.

15. Ibid.

16.   Andrew Zimmerman, "Martindale-Hubbell," Zimmerman's Research Guide, accessed November 19, 2012, law.lexisnexis.com/infopro/ zimmermans/disp.aspx?z=1669.

17.   Paul L. Caron, "The Top 100 Law Reviews," TaxProfBlog, February 7, 2008, accessed April 3, 2013, www.taxprof.typepad.com/taxprof_blog/ 2008/02/the-top-100-law.html.

Chapter 3

"How Do I Copyright My Name?": Answering Legal Reference Questions

A favorite story among librarians of all stripes is the story of the Jesus photo. Here is the version from Bizarre Questions and What Library School Never Taught You (www.bizarrequestions.blogspot.com), where it showed up on April 28, 2008:

> It is a Sunday afternoon in the public library and I am on the reference desk. A nicely dressed man, probably in his mid 40s, comes up to the desk. "Can I help you?" I ask. "Yes," he said. "I'd like to see the photo of Jesus."
>
> I scrutinize his face. I look around for hidden camcorders or some sign that this is a joke. But no. The man is 100 percent serious. So I take a deep breath and say, "Do you mean some of the religious paintings of Jesus?"
>
> "No," he says, looking at me as if I am too stupid to understand the question. "The *photo* of Jesus."
>
> With a perfectly straight face and sincere tone, I say, "Well, that's gonna be hard to come by because Jesus lived 2,000 years ago and the camera was only invented in the 1800s. If I had a photo of Jesus, I'd be very rich because I would've sold it long ago."
>
> "What do you mean?" he asked angrily. "I've seen pictures of Jesus all over the place! I am just asking you to *show me the real one!*"

Patiently, I say, "What you have seen are artistic renditions of Jesus. See, if the artist is white, then Jesus is white with blue eyes. If the artist is Hispanic, then Jesus is Hispanic-looking. If the artist is black, then Jesus is black. See how that works?"

I try to allow him to save face. "Would you like to see a book that has a lot of paintings of Jesus in it instead?" I ask him.

The patron was having none of it. "Look, if you don't have a photo of Jesus you should just say so! I am going to the Christian bookstore! I bet they'll have a picture of Jesus!" And with that statement, he stormed out of the library.

Librarians laugh at such patrons-say-the-funniest-things stories (another good source is www.librarything.com/topic/17962). We laugh guilt-free, knowing the stakes are relatively low when someone is looking for a picture of Jesus. Other patrons, however, are not so risible. They come in needing medical information or help finding a job. Patrons with legal questions have this same sense of urgency. Every day, people need to know how to divorce a spouse, get custody of children, evict a nonpaying tenant (or avoid eviction by a heartless landlord), start a small business, expunge a criminal record, get a significant other out of jail, settle tax liens, restart Social Security or unemployment benefits, or defend against a lawsuit. These are big problems, crises in some cases, especially among those who cannot afford a lawyer. That so many people are self-represented is a crisis in itself, one that has been transforming the legal system for years (see Chapter 9 for more on this).

The stakes are also high for attorneys, who are hired by their clients to stave off these types of threats. Attorneys who fail might face a malpractice lawsuit. Clients sue for malpractice all the time—but the suit is warranted, and the former client will likely win, if the attorney overlooked a key statute or relied on an over-turned case. Judges have even sanctioned attorneys for failing to conduct diligent, thorough legal research,[1] sometimes adding the sanction *on top* of a malpractice award.

The rise of the self-represented and the pressures of legal research make access to information the crux of legal practice. What tools and techniques should librarians use to facilitate this access?

Pro Se Patrons

The technical term for representing oneself in a legal matter is *pro se representation*. Pro se is a Latin phrase meaning "for oneself" or "on one's behalf." A person may be pro se in a civil case as plaintiff or defendant or in a criminal case as a defendant. The right to act pro se dates back to the beginning of the United States with the Judiciary Act of 1789, which provided that "in all the courts of the United States, the parties may plead and manage their own causes personally or by the assistance of counsel."[2] Later, the Sixth Amendment to the Constitution set forth rights related to criminal prosecution—rights that include pro se representation, as the U.S. Supreme Court observed in *Faretta v. California*, 422 U.S. 806 (1975).

In the last 10 years, court systems everywhere have seen an increase in their numbers of pro se litigants. According to a 2009 survey by the Self-Represented Litigation Network, 60 percent of judges nationwide reported such an increase. In Oregon, 65 percent of family law cases involve at least one pro se, and in Maryland, the number is 70 percent. Out of nearly 250,000 child support cases in Texas in 2011, 95 percent involved at least one pro se litigant.[3] For more information on pro se litigants, check out the following websites:

- SelfHelpSupport.org (www.selfhelpsupport.org)

- National Center for State Courts (www.ncsc.org)

- National Association for Court Management
  (www.nacmnet.org)

The trend is not limited to state courts. In 2010, 26 percent of all actions filed in U.S. courts—including a colossal 93 percent of prisoner petitions—were filed by pro se parties.[4] The Legal Services Corporation (LSC), which is the largest provider of civil legal aid for the poor in the U.S., has estimated that four out of every five income-eligible people who apply for assistance are turned away because the LSC lacks the resources to help them all.[5]

So where do pro se clients get the expertise to handle legal matters on their own? From law librarians, of course. They ask us to fill out their forms, summarize the law, tell them what to request in court, explain their rights, or proofread their documents. Some say they need "the law" on a certain topic, not realizing that "the law" is usually a patchwork quilt of statutes, cases, federal or state regulations, and maybe a local ordinance. Moreover, "the law," as a human construct, is subjective, variable, and, in some instances, silent. Try telling that to an overwhelmed pro se.

"Overwhelmed" is a good descriptor. Most of the time, the library is not their first stop on their legal journey. They have tried attorneys (too expensive), legal aid (too busy), and the courthouse staff (too curt). Then someone says to them, "Why don't you try the library?" By then, it is dawning on them that legal action is more burdensome, drawn-out, and nitpicky than they had imagined. And they will tell you about it. For some patrons, the best service you can provide is to listen.

But, don't take it personally if they lash out. In one article in *Legal Reference Services Quarterly*, the law librarian author recalls a patron who had asked for an attorney recommendation. The author tells the patron that he can't give her one, to which she responds in the obscenely negative. After noting that it had been a rational conversation up to that moment, he muses, "She has a point. I wasn't giving her the information she needed. As far as she was concerned, I was just part of the bureaucratic run-around."[6] For a while, I was part of that same run-around with Dan, the patron in search of how to handle his right-of-way situation.

For the most part, however, pro se litigants are earnest and hard-working. Like all library patrons, they need you to point them in the right direction, which you can do after conducting a good reference interview.

The Reference Interview

Most legal information requests fall into one of three categories: reference, research, and referral. In each category, requests can be further divided into six types: laws, regulation, cases, subject, procedure, and location.

Reference requests are narrow questions with specific answers. Usually, those answers can be found in a matter of minutes. *Research* questions are more in-depth—answered in an hour or two, maybe more—and give librarians an opportunity to teach the patron how to identify and use information sources. *Referral* requests are those best handled by an organization other than the library. Some examples of each are:[7]

Reference
Laws: Has H.R. 274 been signed into law?
Regulation: I need the current New Jersey Standards for Licensure of Long Term Care Facilities.
Cases: Where can I get the text of *Roe v. Wade*?
Subject: What does the term *pendente lite* mean?
Procedure: What is Rule 4.2 of New Jersey Civil Procedure?
Location: Where can I find the laws of New York State?

Research

Laws: Is there a law against owning elephants?

Regulation: What are the legal requirements for transporting formaldehyde?

Cases: I need to locate cases on age discrimination.

Subject: What major federal legislation is pending concerning the environment?

Procedure: What are the basic procedures for suing in small claims court?

Location: What legal sources are available on the internet?

Referral

Laws: I need a copy of the French motor vehicle laws … in English.

Regulation: What licenses will I need to export formaldehyde to Russia?

Cases: Can I sue my employer for discrimination because I was passed over for promotion?

Subject: Is my employer obligated to give me vacation time?

Procedure: Can you help me calculate the proper amount of child support I should be getting?

Location: Who is the best divorce attorney in the state of New Jersey?

Pro se patrons, as I have said, don't tend to know much about the law. What brings them to the library is a need to take action—say, to respond to a complaint or administrative notice (see Appendix A for a list of actual law library patron questions). The best way to help them is to stay focused on that action. Following are some questions to ask:

Type of Information

- Do you have specific citations or a general subject?

- What is the original source of your question?

- What is the purpose of this research?
- What do you already know about this topic?

Quantity of Information

- Do you need a document summary or the full text?
- Do you need plain language or professional legal texts?
- What is the deadline for this research?

Legal Details

- Do you need laws, regulations, cases, procedures, news, or history?
- What jurisdiction do you need: federal, state, local, or international?
- Do you need the law (i.e., statute or regulation) as it was passed or as it stands today?

Most patrons can answer questions about type and quantity of information. The legal details, however, confuse them. One strategy is to ask if the research is being driven by a printed document such as a legislative bill, court paper, school assignment, textbook, or newspaper article. If so, ask to see the document. You might find clues to help guide the research, such as a bill sponsor, case or statute citation, or court rule reference. When patrons give you incomplete information such as a partial citation or a statute's common name (e.g., ERISA, Megan's Law, Title IX), ask for the context of the question. Patrons who want Title IX, for example, usually mean the Educational Amendments of 1972, which means they are likely researching sex discrimination in public schools. When the patron asks you to "look up the law on" a topic, ask her to brainstorm keywords or synonyms. You can match these terms with index headings in an encyclopedia, digest, or treatise. Different resources use different terms for the same topic (e.g., *children* could appear under *infants, minors,* or *parent and child*) so have a legal thesaurus handy. A good one is *Burton's Legal Thesaurus.*

Finally, for patrons who can't seem to give you any details about their research, suggest that they start with a self-help resource. *Nolo's Essential Guide to Divorce,* for example, is a great book on that topic. State bar associations often publish plain-language materials that are good places to start. For example, the North Carolina Bar Association website (www.ncbar.org) offers free pamphlets discussing the law on home-buying, domestic violence, worker's compensation, living wills, bankruptcy, auto accidents, and other topics.

Nine Ways Public Librarians Can Prepare for Legal Reference

1. Read a how-to book on legal research (see Chapter 9).
2. Know several academic law library websites to which you can refer patrons (see Chapter 9).
3. Learn the fine points of legal citation. Two good beginner sources are Introduction to Basic Legal Citation (www.law.cornell.edu/citation) and Bluebook 101 (lib.law.washington.edu/content/guides/bluebook-101).[8]
4. Learn which branches of government—legislative, judicial, or regulatory—are responsible for which types of legal issues. This helps you know what type of document to help your patron locate: statute, case, or regulation.
5. Know the U.S. court structure, as well as the court structure for your state. For U.S. courts, see www.uscourts.gov/FederalCourts.aspx. For all 50

states, see www.ncsc.org/Information-and-Resources/Browse-by-State/State-Court-Websites.aspx.

6. Know the basics of articulating a legal issue. What jurisdiction is involved: federal or state? Is it a civil or criminal matter? Who are the parties and what relief is sought (money, injunction, etc.)? Is the issue a substantive or procedural one? Asking patrons such questions often jump-starts the research process.

7. Speaking of procedural issues, learn to recognize them. Then refer patrons to your state's Rules of Civil Procedure, which are found either in the state statutes or in a separate volume owned by any law library. Examples include:
   - How do I sue someone?
   - I just got sued. What do I do?
   - What should my documents look like?
   - I didn't show up for my trial because I never got the notice. What should I do?

8. Know where to find judicial forms. For federal, go to www.uscourts.gov/FormsAndFees.aspx. For state, go to www.professional.getlegal.com/research.

9. Know when and where to refer people who need to talk to an attorney. Signs that they need a referral are when they avoid doing their own research or when, after listening to their tortuous story for 10 minutes, you have only a fleeting notion of what they want. Good places to refer those in need of an attorney are the bar association lawyer referral service, nonprofit legal aid organization (most have income requirements), and law school clinics (most law schools have at least one).

Unauthorized Practice of Law

A special concern for law librarians serving the public is this: How much service can we provide? Suppose a young, well-dressed patron—we'll call him Arthur—walks in and approaches the reference desk. "Hello," Arthur says. "My wife and I are getting a divorce, and neither of us can afford a lawyer. I've decided to write the separation agreement for us. Do you have any examples I could look at?"

As you talk to Arthur more, you learn that he and his wife have no children and don't own a house. Since they have no major property to divide, the divorce should be a simple one. You have looked up divorce statutes for many patrons in the past, so you know that a separation agreement is not essential to divorce in your state, and you want to save Arthur a lot of unnecessary work. You casually mention what you know about separation agreements.

Stop right there. You may have just given legal advice. I know what you're thinking: You're not a lawyer, and you never said you were a lawyer, and the conversation occurred in a library, not a law office. Those are excellent points, but they may not matter. If the patron reasonably believed you were a lawyer and reasonably believed your response created an attorney–client relationship, then a jury could find you guilty of unauthorized practice of law (UPL). This is not as far-fetched as it sounds. In one of the most-cited articles on this topic, Yvette Brown points out that pro se users are "unaware of the fundamental differences between the services of an attorney and the services of a librarian," a confusion that could lead to the accidental transmission of legal advice.[9] Having been asked by dozens of end-of-their-rope patrons to tell them what to do or to help them fill out a form, I agree that the boundaries are not as clear to them as they are to me.

The concept of UPL first appeared in the library literature in the mid-1970s and has been frequently discussed, though infrequently

agreed upon, ever since. As early as 1971, librarians were express-
ing their reticence to help pro se patrons: "I would not close off our
library to lay persons and say, 'no lay person can come in,' except
that I do not believe I have the same obligation to them that I do to
the members of the bar."[10] In 1976, Robert Begg took this senti-
ment a step further, arguing that public patrons should pay fees,
receive limited service, and be given "the old run-around."[11] (I was
unfamiliar with this article when I helped Dan.) More severe still
is a 1983 article by C. C. Kirkwood and Tim Watts, who feel that pro
se users should not be helped at all unless a specific institutional
policy requires it. In their view, a librarian must be prepared to
control the flow of information to a user, "turning it on and off like
a spigot." They note that law librarians can't "hide the law," but neither should they be "spreading the word."[12]

I have watched this ill-disposed attitude on the faces of librarian
colleagues, seen it in their bowed heads and crossed arms, and
heard it in their not-too-friendly voices. Even I don't always leap at
the chance to help public patrons. Most law librarians, when asked
about this reluctance, would probably say they don't have the time
or resources for pro se assistance. Some would agree with the
librarian quoted in the previous paragraph who does not see "the
same obligation to them" as to "members of the bar."

I believe there are other reasons, unstated but no less com-
pelling. One is arrogance. Many law librarians have both library science and law degrees, and even though they don't practice law, they
buy into the exalted self-image that is part of legal culture. They
know they are capable of the same types of complex research that
lawyers do, and they don't feel challenged by someone who just
needs a form. Another is desensitization. Those in crisis-solving
professions—doctors, nurses, EMTs, lawyers, engineers, even
politicians—often fail to mirror their clients' urgency because they
have usually seen and handled worse.

Law librarians make this mistake as well. We serve hundreds of patrons a day, all needing the same things: musty court cases, byzantine forms, guidelines for this, and rules for that. It is easy to forget that we may be the only law librarian a patron ever encounters, and that the patron's problem is real and scary and all-consuming to that person, even if it is routine work to us. We have an ethical obligation to provide all the assistance we can while staying clear of UPL violations.

According to contemporary scholars, though, avoiding UPL is actually a cinch. Paul Healey, one of the leading writers on this topic, believes that "the risk of liability arising out of reference interactions is almost nonexistent"—a technical possibility, perhaps, but not a practical one.[13] In other words, "no librarian will ever be prosecuted for unauthorized practice of law while engaging in normal reference activities."[14] What are "normal reference activities"? To me, they include:

- Helping patrons find primary or secondary sources
- Explaining the format or use of a source
- Defining legal terms
- Interpreting citations
- Advising on the research process
- Interpreting a case or statute in the abstract (i.e., without relating it to the patron's situation)

A comparison of what non-lawyer librarians can and cannot do is found in Table 3.1.[15]

Healy advises librarians to do what we do, use reasonable care, and be clear about boundaries. If we do that, he believes, UPL will be nothing to worry about. Though I agree with Healy, it is still important to be well-informed on the UPL issue. Also, any law

Table 3.1   What Non-Lawyer Librarians Can and Cannot Do

Legal Reference (What Librarians Should Do)	Legal Advice (What Librarians Should Not Do)
- Recommend law books on particular subjects, including books that will explain the law and procedures of the courts, and demonstrate how to use them effectively by explaining the indexes and tables of contents.	- Offer an opinion as to how a user's specific legal problem should be handled.
- Recommend law books that provide forms.	- Recommend a specific legal form, explain how to fill in the form, or fill out a legal form for the user. (It is permissible to refer users to form books. The user will need to ultimately decide whether to use those forms or not.) - Write a brief, prepare a will, or draft a contract.
- Help find the broad definition of legal words or phrases, usually by using sources such as *Black's Law Dictionary*, *Cal. Jur. 3rd*, *Words and Phrases*, etc.	- Interpret any legal document from a court or an attorney.
- Suggest search terms to employ when using indexes or finding tools. - Perform an online search to provide the user with information that may be relevant to his legal question.	- Identify any single law as *the* statute (or regulation, or case) that will answer the user's legal question.
- Teach legal research techniques such as the use of digests and *Shepard's*.	- Help a person by interpreting the law (statutes, regulations, or cases).
- Locate biographical information about attorneys and judges.	- Recommend an attorney or law firm.

library serving the public should have a written policy posted where patrons can read it. Here is an example.

A Message to Our Users About
Legal Reference Questions

It is unlawful for members of the Library staff to help users interpret legal materials they read or to advise them how the law might apply to their situation because these actions would constitute the unauthorized practice of law. It would also require an amount of personal service that a staff of our size cannot provide if we are still to carry out other duties. For those reasons, our staff must limit themselves to advising you which materials might be helpful to you, where they are located, and how to find information in them. Please do not think our staff is being uncooperative when they suggest that you interpret the materials you read for yourself and make your own decisions as to how the material you have read applies to your legal problem. Our staff will be happy to help you find the materials you need, and to show you how to use the various legal publications.

If you need further help to solve your legal problem, you may wish to consult one of the following legal service organizations:

[LIST YOUR LOCAL LEGAL SERVICE PROVIDERS HERE][16]

Another example, from the Connecticut State Library:

Law and Legislative Reference (LLR)
Unit Legal Reference Policy

Because library staff members are not attorneys they cannot offer individual guidance in matters involving litigation or legal forms, and they cannot offer legal advice or any interpretation of the law or legal terms.

- Interpretation is defined as the explanation of what is not immediately plain, explicit, or unmistakable.
- Although staff members will be as helpful as possible in locating and providing necessary legal materials, it is the responsibility of the patron to research his or her own legal issues and come to his or her own conclusions about how the law applies to particular situations.

- LLR staff cannot identify any single law as *the* statute (or regulation, or case) that will answer the patron's legal question.
- LLR staff may suggest sources and explain the organization and format of those sources to in-house patrons who are attempting to devise a search strategy.
- Staff may assist patrons in the use of catalogs, indexes, and research guides to identify and locate pertinent library and archival resources; assist in the use the collections and electronic reference resources; and assist with the operation of photo-copiers and microform equipment.
- Staff may direct patrons in the use of all Connecticut statute compilations and supple-ments to determine public act numbers for leg-islative histories.

The Law and Legislative Reference Unit staff responds to telephone, letter, email and fax inquiries that pertain to legal and legislative issues and can be answered from sources within the collection.

- LLR staff may help to find the broad definition of legal words or phrases, usually by using sources such as legal dictionaries and encyclopedias.
- LLR staff may read short quotes from legal materials when the patron has a specific citation (time and policy permitting).
- LLR staff may locate biographical information about attorneys and judges.
- LLR staff may help locate legislative or other back-ground reports or law journal articles, which pro-vide the patron with information that may be relevant to his or her legal question.

- LLR staff may take requests for copies of Connecticut legislative histories when the patron has a specific Public Act number or numbers.
- LLR staff may advise patrons to consult an attorney but they cannot recommend a specific attorney or law firm.[17]

Extreme Patrons

A patron wants to look up something she "heard somewhere"—say, that the Fifteenth Amendment is due to expire soon. Another patron needs to know how to "officially" copyright his name. (In the library visitor log, he had drawn a © beside his signature.) Still another patron claims to be a Sovereign Citizen.[18] She flouts the library's policy of showing a driver's license at sign-in by handing over a typewritten card, laminated and with her picture on it, from the "Republic of the United States." Except she doesn't think she is flouting the policy; she thinks she is adhering to it. Her card, she claims, excuses her from paying any debt, including income tax. She says she achieved this status by reclaiming her "straw man"— a paper-only alter ego created when a person's birth certificate is issued—and canceling the straw man's debts she had unwittingly assumed.

Librarians have faced extreme patrons as long as there have been libraries. Some, like the Sovereign Citizens, are a "growing domestic threat" (see the FBI's report at www.fbi.gov/stats-services/publications/law-enforcement-bulletin/september-2011/sovereign-citizens). Most, however, are simply misguided, angry, stubborn, or naïve. Because legal questions often involve money, freedom, or life itself (remember Terri Schiavo?), law librarians see more than their share of anger and stubbornness. Because the law is Gordian, we also deal with lots and lots of confusion. Are there special techniques for handling such patrons?

In 2004, two librarians, Amy Hale-Janeke and Sharon Blackburn, addressed this question in a speech at the annual meeting of the American Association of Law Librarians.[19] First, they said, law librarians should treat every question seriously and every patron with respect, even the weird ones. Clarify the question by saying, for example, "Could you tell me more? I'm not sure I understand." Focus on the question, not the patron's demeanor. If the patron seems sane (i.e., not rambling, disheveled and smelly, prone to outbursts, or talking to unseen companions) then do a regular reference interview.

If the patron *is* insane,[20] still treat him/her with respect, but realize your priorities have changed. Your goal is not to find information—the patron likely won't even look at it—but to avoid a confrontation. Keep your voice even, your gaze steady, and your movements undemonstrative. Don't argue with the patron: You'll frustrate yourself and make him mad, which can lead to violence. Accept his reality. You can even enter it a little. Give him a book and say it's a secret book, or join her briefly in an absurd digression before steering the talk back to the original request. Maintain boundaries—no touching, no personal questions, no breaking library policy—and call a colleague over if necessary. Above all, understand that you can't help everyone. Insane patrons often have insane requests, and you are not a failure as a librarian for not meeting such requests.

Law Firm Reference

Library school reference classes assume that you, the librarian, know more about the resources than your patrons. In public and academic libraries, this is mostly true. In law firms, it is not. After 3 years of law school plus any number of years practicing law, attorneys know how to research, and they know the major primary and secondary sources. They know them like old friends and call them by nicknames (see Chapter 2). They even know where most of the books are, because they have used them over and over or because the books are shelved in their offices. Law firms tend to have decentralized collections. At one of my firms, for example, the main library was on one floor, litigation materials on another floor, and corporate law materials on a third floor. Other titles were shelved in hallways, conference rooms, or an attorney's office. (Surprisingly, this arrangement works. Just note in the catalog that the location for Title X is Attorney Y, and if someone else ever needs it, you know right where it is.)

How do you help such high-functioning, self-reliant patrons?

Types of Requests

For starters, the fact that lawyers *can* do all their own research doesn't mean that they will. Some attorneys, especially senior ones, see research as a low-level function, and not something they prefer to spend their time on. From a client's standpoint, this is a good approach. Suppose you are an executive with a Fortune 500 company, and you hire attorney Smith to handle a legal matter. Smith's billing rate is $600 an hour. Do you want Smith to spend those hours developing a strategy for your defense, or looking up cases in the library?

Right. Let Smith do what he does. *You* can look up the cases. This is the biggest difference between reference in law firms and public libraries: Pro se patrons rarely know what they need; law firm patrons usually do. Attorneys will give you a list of citations to cases, statutes, regulations, articles, whatever, and all you have to do is retrieve the documents. Sometimes they give you wrong or incomplete citations, and sometimes all they have is a case name or part of a name. Typical requests are along the lines of: "I'm looking for a case, came out in the last few years, the plaintiff is Jones. Or maybe it was the defendant." When you get this type of request, ask what the case is about. This will help you narrow down the five or six—or 6,000—cases involving a party named Jones.

Citations are tricky, even for experienced attorneys. Remember writing papers in MLA format? Your handbook might be cotton-field-white with creases, yet you would *still* have to look up how to lay out the title page or cite a personal interview. Legal format is just as obscure. Attorneys cite cases and statutes all the time, but they struggle with the more obscure formats.

Become an expert in citation and formatting. This is important because some judges will reject an improperly formatted brief. At the very least, the judge will be annoyed, which makes it harder for your attorney to win the case. At one firm, I was sometimes asked to proofread the citations in appellate briefs. Secretaries proofed the grammar and spelling, but with citations, they yielded to my expertise, as did the lawyers. You can make yourself indispensable with this skill.

Another major difference is that many law firm requests do not involve legal information. Instead, you will field requests for medical information, business information, or news articles. Databases are fine for most articles, though there are exceptions. A 30-year-old newspaper article (which I have been asked for) will not appear in most databases, so you might have to find it on microfilm. Also, databases tend to omit charts, tables, and pictures, so if graphics are why the attorney wants the article (another request I have often had), you will have to get creative. Of course, the attorney may want to frame a full newspaper front page from 3 months ago because it pictures a client—or himself. Do the best you can with this.

For business information, see Chapter 7. For medical information, here are a few starting points:

- Lisa Ennis and Nicole Mitchell, *The Accidental Health Sciences Librarian* (Information Today, Inc., 2010)

- Medical Library Association (www.mlanet.org)

- U.S. National Library of Medicine (www.nlm.nih.gov)

- Medical Libraries on the Web
  (www.lib.uiowa.edu/hardin/hslibs)

Managing the Requests

Public librarians are usually asked to locate information for patrons on the spot. In a law firm, most requests are not immediate, but they do have deadlines. If the requester does not give you a deadline, ask for one. Also, if the request is for in-depth research, ask what the requester is working on. Appellate brief? Internal memo? Article for the bar association rag? Conference presentation? School paper for the requester's daughter? (Don't laugh; I've had this one, too.) The answer will affect not only your timeline but also the depth and kind of information you return. Make sure you know how each requester likes to have information sent. Email? Hard copy? If you don't know, ask. And here is a nice touch: If you find a lot of information—say, three or more documents—include a cover letter summarizing each. Busy attorneys love time-savers like this.

Another major consideration is client billing. If the research is for a specific client, then the firm might bill that client for your time. If so, you would need to track your work (most firms bill in 6-minute increments). Also, if you use Westlaw, LexisNexis, or some other database, you may be able to pass along this cost to the client. Be sure to clear this with the requesting attorney in advance.

Information currency is something else to consider. Law changes daily, yet attorneys don't always need the latest information. For background knowledge, an old article or treatise works as well as a new one. Attorneys get used to certain titles, and even when the publisher stops updating it, they will want to keep using that title. Is this legal malpractice? Not if they use Westlaw or

LexisNexis to update the authorities they find in the outdated text (see Chapter 5). Be sure to ask the requester how current the information needs to be.

Summer Associates

Each year, many law firms hire law school student interns. They are sometimes called *summer associates*. The biggest firms might hire 10 or 12 of these interns every summer, some of whom will likely be offered full-time positions when they graduate from law school.

Summer associates work alongside senior attorneys on actual cases, often doing all the research for the cases. As inexperienced researchers, they need guidance, not just document retrieval. Two strategies you can suggest are secondary sources or the "one good case" method.

The first thing summer associates want to do is hop on Westlaw or Lexis, plug in keywords, and pull up cases. They will not start with secondary sources because these are scarcely taught in law school. Experienced practitioners, however, often start with secondary sources, which collect and summarize leading authorities. Teach your summer associates to do likewise.

Inexperienced researchers like summer associates often try to find everything at once. Through broad keyword searches on Westlaw or Lexis, they cast their net wide, hoping to bring in dozens of useful cases at once. Encourage them instead to find "one good case" (i.e., a known case on point that can be used, through citators or the West Key Number System, to find other relevant cases). How can a summer associate find this "one good case"?

- Word of mouth, or asking the supervising attorney to recommend one
- Secondary sources

- Annotated statutes, or finding a relevant statute (if there is one) in an annotated code and looking through the case notes

Law Firm Culture

Some attorneys love research and will be your biggest patrons. Others hate it and will never darken your door. Learn which is which. Also learn which high-ranking attorneys will talk to you directly and which leave the interaction with you to other support staff.

Remember Gabriel, the grumpy managing partner from Chapter 1? Through Preston, the office administrator, Gabriel had asked me to do some research. A question came up about the research, so I emailed my question to Gabriel. Within minutes, Preston, not Gabriel, called me with the answer. Some time later, I had another question for Gabriel, so I emailed him again. This time, Preston responded in 60 seconds. "Did you just send Gabriel *another* email?" he asked.

Now, I get that Gabriel was a busy man, but in the time it took him to forward my emails to Preston, he could have answered me himself. Why didn't he? A law firm caste system, I suppose. Preston implied as much as we discussed my breach of etiquette. "I know the politics of the place," he said, meaning that he could help me a lot if I would let him. I did, and he turned out to be a valuable advocate for the library.

Every law firm has a personality. Learn yours. Maintain whatever illusions you are asked to maintain, at least until you have earned enough respect to shatter them. When I had my wall-building discussion with Preston, I had not been at this firm long. Later, once I had proven myself, those walls came down. I started going to attorneys' offices, stopping them in the halls, asking them what they were working on and how the library could help. I got a lot more business this way, but more important, I won the attorneys' trust.

In law firms, librarians, like secretaries and paralegals, will always be support staff, but that doesn't mean you have to act like it. Present yourself as an intellectual equal, as qualified as any attorney to discuss research matters—in other words, a colleague. Sooner or later, they'll treat you like one.

Listen to Your Patrons

Different patrons require different service approaches. To know what your patrons need, listen to them. Too often, when a patron starts talking, our minds skip ahead to sources and strategies, and we don't even hear the whole issue. We avoid *active listening*.[21] Or, we respond with why we can't help—the question is too in-depth, the information doesn't exist, we can't give legal advice, blah blah blah—instead of exploring how we can. Legal reference has unique considerations, but none should outweigh the ethical obligation of all librarians: to "provide the highest level of service to all library users through appropriate and usefully organized resources; equitable service policies; equitable access; and accurate, unbiased, and courteous responses to all requests."[22]

Endnotes

1. For a thorough discussion of this, see Marguerite L. Butler, "Rule 11 Sanctions and a Lawyer's Failure to Conduct Competent Legal Research," *Capital University Law Review* 29 (2002): 681–717.
2. 1 Stat. 73, 92.
3. Texas Access to Justice Commission, "Pro Se Statistics," accessed November 20, 2012, www.texasatj.org/files/file/3ProSeStatistics Summary.pdf.
4. "Civil Pro Se And Non-Pro Se Filings, by District, During the 12-Month Period Ending September 30, 2010," Administrative Office of the U.S. Courts, accessed November 20, 2012, www.uscourts.gov/uscourts/Statistics/JudicialBusiness/2010/tables/S23Sep10.pdf.
5. Paula L. Hannaford-Agor, "Helping the Pro Se Litigant: A Changing Landscape," *Court Review* 39, no. 4 (2003): 8–16.

6. Mike Chiorazzi, "Just Another Wednesday Night: And You May Ask Yourself, Well, How Did I Get Here?", *Legal Reference Services Quarterly* 18, no. 4 (2001): 1.

7. Examples courtesy of the Morris County Library in Whippany, NJ. Lynne Lover, "Legal Reference: Tips and Techniques," Highlands Regional Library Cooperative, February 11, 2000, accessed November 20, 2012, www.gti.net/mocolib1/demos/legaltip.html.

8. *The Bluebook: A Uniform System of Citation* is the manual followed by all U.S. and state courts. There are alternatives, most notably *The University of Chicago Manual of Legal Citation*, also called The Maroon Book. It is not on the verge of replacing its cyan counterpart. I have never used it, and no one I know has ever used it. I don't even know the difference between the two.

9. Yvette Brown, "From the Reference Desk to the Jail House: Unauthorized Practice of Law and Librarians," *Legal Reference Services Quarterly* 13, no. 4 (1994): 31–45.

10. "Reader Services in Law Libraries—A Panel," *Law Library Journal* 64, no. 4(1971): 486–506.

11. Robert T. Begg, "The Reference Librarian and the Pro Se Patron," *Law Library Journal* 69 (1976): 26–32.

12. Kirkwood, C. C., and Tim Watts, "Legal Reference Service: Duties v. Liabilities," *Legal Reference Services Quarterly* 3 (Summer 1983): 67–82.

13. Paul D. Healey, "Pro Se Users, Reference Liability, and the Unauthorized Practice of Law: Twenty-Five Selected Readings," *Law Library Journal* 94, no. 1 (2002): 133.

14. Ibid., 134.

15. Joan Allen-Hart, "Legal Reference v. Legal Advice," *Locating the Law: A Handbook for Non-Law Librarians*, 5th ed. (Los Angeles: Southern California Association of Law Librarians, 2011): 49.

16. Ibid.

17. "Law and Legislative Reference (LLR) Unit Legal Reference Policy," Connecticut State Library, September 28, 2010, accessed November 20, 2012, www.cslib.org/legalref.htm.

18. See "Domestic Terrorism: The Sovereign Citizen Movement," Federal Bureau of Investigation, April 13, 2010, accessed November 20, 2012, www.fbi.gov/news/stories/2010/april/sovereigncitizens_041310.

19. See Rhonda Schwartz, "Say What?! How to Handle Reference Questions from Patrons Who Seemingly Inhabit an Alternate Universe," *AALL Spectrum*, Sept./Oct. 2004, pp. 20–21.

20. For advice on dealing with mental disabilities, see www.nami.org or www.nmha.org.

21. "Active Listening," Conflict Research Consortium, 1998, accessed November 20, 2012, www.colorado.edu/conflict/peace/treatment/activel.htm.

22. "Code of Ethics of the American Library Association," *Intellectual Freedom Manual*, 8th ed., January 22, 2008, accessed November 20, 2012, www.ifmanual.org/codeethics.

Chapter 4

The Art of Hanging Loose(leaf) in an Uptight World

This is a good time to tell you more about my first law library job. The firm was Haynsworth Sinkler Boyd (HSB), P.A., located in Columbia, South Carolina. At the time, HSB had three offices, all in the Palmetto State[1]: Columbia, Charleston, and Greenville. It has since opened two more offices (in Myrtle Beach, South Carolina, and Washington, DC).

I was hired as the library clerk. At the time, the library had probably seven or eight thousand volumes, most of them residing in the main library. The rest were shelved in hallways, conference rooms, or the offices of the attorneys who used them the most. My boss, the librarian, was actually a long-serving paralegal thrust into the role of library caretaker. She handled most of the research questions, as well as maintaining an active caseload, mostly in the Charleston office. I did some basic research—finding documents by citation, for example—and also reshelved books, processed invoices, and took care of other housekeeping duties. However, my biggest responsibility, and one of the biggest responsibilities in any law library, was filing updates in the many looseleaf volumes.

Looseleafs Defined

Chapters 1 and 2 discuss looseleafs as a special type of secondary source. A fuller definition comes from the Georgetown Law Library:

A looseleaf service is a popular type of legal source which brings together a variety of types of information concerning a particular topic or area of law. A looseleaf service is so called because it is made up of pages or pamphlets filed in looseleaf binders, often a multi-volume set. This format allows current information to be easily added to the existing materials. The ease of updating the binders allows supplementation to be added frequently, even weekly in some cases.[2]

Looseleafs are common in practice areas that rely heavily on statutes and administrative regulations, such as environmental law, labor law, tax law, and securities law. They contain both full-text primary materials—cases, statutes, regs—and some that are summarized. Looseleafs also contain secondary material (e.g., explanatory text).

Looseleaf binders come in a variety of styles. Some are 3-ring, 4-ring, or 5-ring binders. Other binders use a D-ring or arch ring, while another common type is the compression-post or post-hole binder. This type is opened by pulling a tab-like ring to loosen a post attached to the top cover of the binder. The entire cover is lifted off, removing the post from the center hole of the three-hole-punched pages.

The page formats are also varied. Depending on the title and publisher, each page may bear the publication number, title, volume number, page number, paragraph or section number, supplement number, date of supplement (for supplemented pages), or original publication date (for pages that have not been supplemented). Pagination may be continuous (1 to end) or may track specific changes (8-1 through 8-24) and special sections (Table of Cases 1-45, Table of Statutes 1-19, Index 1-60). The supplements also may take different forms:

- Interfiled single sheets
- Pamphlets filed as a unit at the end or beginning of the binder
- Pamphlets filed together as a unit within the binder (i.e., new chapters)[3]

There are three reasons to use a looseleaf. First, it's convenient having primary and secondary material together in a single set of volumes. Second, looseleafs are updated frequently, meaning they are a good source of up-to-date information. Law-related blogs and other websites can of course be updated daily, sometimes more than once a day; however, as unedited forums, they often sacrifice quality for speed. Looseleafs are the only type of publication to achieve both. Third, as a feature of their editorial quality, looseleafs have comprehensive indexes and finding aids, making it easy to locate information.

Varieties of Looseleafs

There are two main types of looseleafs: interfiled and newsletter. An *interfiled looseleaf*, also called a true looseleaf, contains both primary and secondary material (as described in the previous section). Individual pages in each binder are removed and replaced with each supplement, allowing changes in the law to be incorporated into the text. This format eliminates the need to consult a pocket part or supplemental pamphlet. (See the discussion of statutes in Chapter 2.) Each supplement comes with a sheet of filing instructions, indicating which existing pages are replaced by which new pages. Common Clearing House (CCH; www.cch.com) is the leading publisher of interfiled looseleafs.

The most current material appears in the main binders of the title. As more cases are decided and statutes and regulations are codified, this material would outgrow the binders if it were not periodically culled. Once or twice a year, the publisher sends a separate softcover binder called a *transfer binder*. Older documents—the instructions will tell you which ones—may be removed from the main binders and placed into the transfer binder, freeing up space in the main binders. The transfer binder is then shelved as a permanent volume.

In a *newsletter looseleaf*, individual pages are not replaced. Rather, each installment is issued as a topical newsletter. Newsletters will be discussed in detail later in this chapter.

There is a third less-common type of looseleaf: the *newsletter hybrid*. Supplements of this type include interfiled pages *and* a topical newsletter, though a newsletter may not arrive with each supplement. An example is *Tax Management Memorandum*, which libraries receive as part of their subscription to the Bureau of National Affairs' (BNA) *U.S. Income Portfolios Library*, a series of 200 spiral-bound notebooks that provide in-depth guidance on every aspect of U.S. tax law. Updates to the notebooks arrive every 2 weeks, while the *Memorandum* is published monthly. BNA also publishes the *Estates, Gifts and Trusts Portfolios Library*, which includes the monthly *Estates, Gifts and Trusts Journal*, and the *Foreign Income Portfolios Library*, accompanied by the *International Journal*.

Finally, some treatises are commonly called looseleafs because they are printed on loose, three-hole-punched pages gathered in a ringed binder. Replacement pages arrive less often than with true looseleafs—usually every 3 to 6 months—and they are interfiled. Remember, however, that a treatise is an in-depth, scholarly examination of an area of law, not an amalgam of primary materials, news, and commentary. The difference is technical and rarely observed by attorneys.

Tips for Using Looseleafs

- Read the directions—often entitled "How to Use This Reporter"—in the front of the first volume. The layout of looseleafs can be confusing, so a few minutes spent reading this prolegomenon will save mistakes and wasted time later.

- Some looseleafs are supplemented with colored pages in the front of a volume. These pages contain *very* new material (i.e., too new to make it into the regular replacement pages). When referring to this kind of volume, check these colored pages first before delving into the volume.

- When you know the specific item you want from a looseleaf, use the publication's finding list and case tables. A finding list is a gathering of documents, usually court decisions and administrative materials, with a reference to their location in the set. Some tax looseleafs, for example, publish tables of tax rulings along with digests of those rulings. Such lists provide the most efficient access to regulations, laws, or decisions.

- When you have a topic but don't know what documents to retrieve, use an index. (Note that some looseleafs have an index *supplement* to update the regular index.)

- Some looseleafs have paragraph numbers as well as page numbers. The indexes for these titles may refer to paragraph numbers or page numbers or both. Know which you are dealing with.

- Looseleafs may be updated weekly, biweekly, monthly, or semiannually. Check the date on the latest filing instructions (kept either at the front of the first volume or the back of the last) for the title's currency. In addition, for many titles, the month and year on which each page was issued is printed on that page, usually in the top or bottom margin.

- Sometimes, as you turn the page in a looseleaf volume, the text on the new page seems not to continue the text on the previous one. This is probably because one or more pages were taken out[4] or misfiled. When you encounter this, simply contact the publisher to ask for replacement pages. If a lot of pages are missing, or there is more than one gap, it may be better to replace *all* the pages in a volume. (This can often be done at no charge.)

- Wondering whether a looseleaf exists on a particular topic? Look at *Legal Looseleafs in Print*, available in hard copy or as a subscription database (www.info sourcespub.com).

Looseleaf Filers

So how do the various new looseleaf pages make it into the binders of the titles they supplement? Someone has to put them there, of course. A looseleaf filer can be a library employee, either full- or part-time. Other libraries, especially in large law firms, use independent contractors. These contractors can be individuals or may be companies with a full suite of library consulting, staffing, and other services. Examples include the Law Library Consultants (www.lawlibraryconsultants.com), AccuFile (www.accufile.com), and Law Library Management (www.lawlib.com).

A good filer is someone who is fast and self-sufficient, can follow directions, and has terrific attention to detail. Oh, and it helps to be long-suffering. Here is how one filer described the situation:

> First, it's certainly not glamorous work, so you can't have a huge ego. Lawyers and staff people may think, "she's only the looseleaf filer." You can't let that bother you, if it does. They will think what they will think; there's nothing you can do about it. I think you need to have a "go with the flow" personality, except here it's "go with the supplement." Sometimes you get through a huge pile, and there's a real feeling of accomplishment. Sometimes you're pulling out and putting in endless single pages and it seems like it's taking forever. But you can't hurry it. Some days things just take longer. That's okay.[5]

I handled the looseleaf filing full-time at HSB under the direction of a part-time librarian. At my next firm, the roles were reversed: I was the full-time librarian with a part-time (8–10 hours a week) filer, Sylvia, who, like most filers, also inserted pocket parts into volumes when necessary. Sylvia was an excellent filer, quick and self-sufficient, though due to the size of the collection, I did a lot of the filing as well. Between the two of us, we kept up. If all the filing had fallen to me, I would have been everlastingly behind, or so it seemed.

I got the chance to test that hunch when Sylvia, who was in her fifties, passed away unexpectedly. Her daughter emailed the news, and I forwarded it to my boss, the library director—I'll call her Georgia—who sent back her sympathies. A few days later, I brought up the need to look for Sylvia's replacement. Georgia surprised me by saying there would be no replacement. Why not? I wanted to know. You don't need one, she replied.

Understand, now, that Georgia did not work in my office; she was at the firm's main office 80 miles away. She did not see the amount of work involved in the filing. How could I do all the filing myself, when I had other duties to keep up with? In particular, I had made a real effort to get more research business from the attorneys, increasing my billable hours by 52 percent in my second year (see Chapter 8 for a discussion of library billings). To me, my boss's refusal to replace Sylvia implied that she had been looking for a chance to get rid of her all along. I argued with Georgia, and she agreed to consider hiring a new filer if I sent her a list of all my library's looseleaf and pocket-parted titles along with the frequency of the updates (weekly, monthly, etc.), plus an estimate of my time in taking care of each one. I compiled this information and sent it to Georgia. Her response: still no filer. I squeezed in all the filing for a few months, and then I left the firm.

Why do I tell this story? Because librarians in law firms and public law libraries do need to track looseleaf filing. Knowing how many hours need to be devoted to filing can help you determine whether existing staff can handle the task or whether you need a dedicated part-time filer. Filers usually also handle pocket parts and shelving of reporter volumes, so be sure to add those duties to your calculations. Another reason for tracking is to help you decide which looseleaf or reporter services to cancel during budget crunches. Those titles that take the most time to update are good candidates.

Table 4.1 is an example of a tracking system for looseleaf filing.

Table 4.1   A Model Tracking System for Looseleaf Filing

Title	# of vols.	Date	Release #	Start time	End time
Standard Federal Tax Reporter	25	8/13/12	v. 99, no. 18	7:15	7:40
Model Agreements for Corporate Counsel	6	8/13/12	2011–2012	7:45	7:55
Bender's Forms for the Civil Practice	40	8/13/12	122	8:05	8:45

How to File Supplements

To file supplements, use the following steps:[6]

1. Check in the supplement. In some libraries, a cataloger does this; in others, the filer takes care of it. Most libraries catalog looseleafs as serials, checking in supplements like issues of magazines.

2. Make sure you received and filed the previous supplement. Do this by checking the catalog or by checking the date on the last filing instructions, which should be saved in the binder.

3. Note whether the current supplement mentions a transfer binder or hardbound volume that has been issued.

4. Collect all the volumes you need (not every volume will have replacement pages) and assemble them in order.

5. Gather your supplies, which could be a rubber finger, a pencil, and gummed reinforcement labels to repair torn pages. Also have your tracking chart handy (see Table 4.1).

6. Find a large table in a quiet spot to work.

7. Review the publisher's filing instructions and verify that you have received all parts of the supplement. Items commonly missing include tabbed divider cards, special

colored updates, and new volume spine labels (necessary when chapters are added or moved around).

8. Separate the filing instructions from the supplement pages.

9. File the supplement pages.

10. Retain the filing instructions in one of the volumes. With most sets, the instructions are filed in the front of Volume 1 or the end of the last volume. Sometimes the publisher provides a tabbed card labeled Last Report Letter, Report Bulletin, or Filing Instructions. Discard the previous set of instructions.

11. Update your tracking chart.

12. Reshelve the volumes.

Sometimes—often, in fact—publishers will make mistakes in the supplements, or the library volumes will be damaged or incomplete. Problems a filer is likely to encounter include:

- Ripped or dilapidated binder covers

- Binder rings not aligned

- Post binders that will not open (usually due to broken posts)

- Binders with too many pages, making them hard to close (this also warps the binder)

- Pages missing from binders

- Holes in pages not aligning with binder rings or posts

- Missing or unfiled supplements

- Missing or erroneous filing instructions

Most of these problems can be solved by contacting the publisher, which will generally replace individual pages or even entire supplements. They will also send new binders to replace damaged ones. If you have a publisher's representative (as is usually the case with Westlaw or LexisNexis), start with that person. Other publishers have an automated process for such claims. CCH, for example, has a website, support.cch.com, for submitting looseleaf claims.

The Future of Looseleafs

In a 2009 survey of law librarians, 61.3 percent reported that they had canceled some or all of their looseleaf services.[7] This 2009 survey is the latest available comprehensive account of cancellations, but more recent anecdotes suggest the trend is only increasing.[8] The chief reason for these cancellations is cost. Law libraries have been hit hard by the recession since 2008 (see Chapter 10), and for looseleafs that are updated four or more times a year, the annual cost can be *two or three times more* for supplements than for a new edition of the title. Of course, not all looseleafs are billed per update; some have a flat annual fee, like any magazine or newspaper.

In addition to cost concerns, many librarians no longer see the value of looseleaf updates. Primary law—statutes, cases, and regulations—make up a significant portion of most titles, and many of these documents can be found online free of charge. Moreover, new documents are available online within hours, as opposed to the weekly, biweekly, or monthly updating of looseleafs. Both staff time and budget dollars can be better used elsewhere.[9]

Speaking of staff time, this is another major concern in maintaining looseleaf subscriptions. Some looseleaf titles comprise 30 or more volumes; some are updated weekly, meaning that as soon as you put away one supplement, another batch arrives and is clamoring for enclosure. In a large library, this filing can easily eat up 20 hours a week. Throw in the time spent dealing with missing pages, damaged binders, and the like (see previous section), as well as inserting pocket parts and shelving new volumes, and you have the makings of a full-time job.

Of course, few libraries have a full-time filer, relying instead on part-timers, contractors, or regular staff to share the load. The cancellation of looseleafs may mean the loss of part-timers and contractors, though other duties can usually be found for these individuals. Ditto for professional librarians who have been helping with filing duties; cancelling looseleafs will allow them to devote more time to reference, instruction, and other patron services. Law firm librarians will feel the push to bill more client hours (see Chapter 8). And publishers, no longer content to support a dying model, will stop publishing looseleaf titles.

Or will they?

My feeling is that treatises are not going anywhere. Recall that many attorneys refer to anything in a three-ring binder as a looseleaf, so in that sense, the genre is not endangered. Westlaw, Lexis, and other databases include full-text treatises, but even GenX practitioners prefer to use the hard copy. The same is true of newsletters, many of which are available in email form. It would seem more efficient to distribute an electronic newsletter than to route a print copy, but email often sits in recipients' inboxes, unread, like so much spam, making it a waste of money. At least the print copy has to be handled, checked off, and sent on its way.

True looseleafs, however, are in jeopardy, at least in their current form. Westlaw has begun converting some looseleaf titles to a pamphlet format, ostensibly in response to customer feedback, though some librarians doubt this rationale.[10] Similarly, one blogger has noted that looseleafs could be released as hardcover books with yearly supplements, "as is already done by a number of British and American publishers."[11] Another solution is to remove from the looseleaf primary law materials that can easily be obtained online. This would also reduce filing time and possibly the cost of supplementation.

The more noteworthy publishing trend is to offer the content of true looseleaf services in electronic formats. Online looseleafs are automatically updated, thus eliminating the need to file supplements and the problems with missing pages, damaged binders, or any of the other annoyances. Moreover, electronic versions can take advantage of hypertext links, allowing publishers to either integrate materials from their own database systems or link to materials available freely elsewhere.[12] CCH has done a fantastic job of digitizing its looseleaf content with Intelliconnect (www.cch group.com/intelliconnect), CCH Internet Research Network (www.business.cch.com/network for subscribers-only), and other platforms.

These platforms, however, do pose some challenges for librarians. One important issue is the way in which online looseleafs are licensed. All the attorneys in a single office can share one copy of a print title, while for electronic titles publishers base their charges on the number of potential (not actual) users. This can get costly. Before negotiating with the publisher, decide which members of the office *must* have access to the product; these are the ones who will appear on the license. Don't be swayed by attorneys who say, "Well, I occasionally have a tax question, so it would be nice to have access." This is one time to rely on your good relationship, if you have developed one, with the firm's administrators, especially the managing partner. It is those people's job to rein in free-spenders, not yours, and they will be glad to do it. Why? They will be impressed with your dedication to the firm's bottom line. (See Chapter 8 for more discussion on building a relationship with firm management.)

Newsletters

Chapter 1 discussed scholarly law journals, usually called *law reviews*, while Chapter 2 dealt with the multitudinous nonscholarly serials common in law libraries. A final type of nonscholarly serial is the *newsletter*. As I mentioned earlier in this chapter, newsletters are often categorized as looseleafs, though I never thought of them this way. Some newsletters publish substantive articles in addition to case summaries and news reports. Some are national, like *Bankruptcy Law Reporter*, which summarizes bankruptcy-related cases before federal trial and appellate courts (Figure 4.1). Others have a regional focus, like *North Carolina Employment Law Letter*, which summarizes labor and employment cases in North Carolina state and federal courts (store.hrhero.com/ncemp). The directory *Legal Newsletters in Print* (www.infosourcespub.com/book6.cfm) lists over 2,200 newsletters from over 600 publishers. Here is a sample entry:

> *Electronic Commerce & Law Report*
> Publ. Co.: The Bureau of National Affairs, Inc.
> 1231 25th Street NW
> Washington, DC 20037
> (202) 452-4200; (800) 372-1033
> Fax: (202) 822-8092
> Email: lgallagh@bna.com
> URL: www.bna.com
> Mng. Editor: Thomas O'Toole
> Publisher: Paul N. Wojcik
> Began 4/96; 48x/yr.; $1,048, $829-electronic; 28pp.; 8.5
>   x 11; hole-punched; free binder; annual index; back
>   issues avail.; CCC.
> Formerly: *BNA's Electronic Information Policy & Law*
> *Report*
> On Internet: www.bna.com
> Covers developing law as it concerns electronic infor-
>   mation. Main focus is legal issues surrounding
>   content and its distribution in the wide array of

BNA's
Bankruptcy Law Reporter™

VOL. 24, NO. 30   PAGES 989–1024   AUGUST 2, 2012

HIGHLIGHTS

Debt Nondischargeable Due to Indifference to Partner's Securities Fraud
A bankruptcy court did not err in concluding that a real estate developer/financier's debts to nine creditors were nondischargeable under Bankruptcy Code Section 523(a) based on his vicarious liability for his partner's securities fraud, the U.S. Court of Appeals for the Eighth Circuit holds. **Page 996**

Ch. 7 Debtor Is Not Entitled to Post-Petition Appreciation in Assets
A bankruptcy court did not err in concluding that a Chapter 7 debtor exempted only an interest in oil and gas leases rather than in the asset itself and, thus, was entitled to only the dollar amount listed as wildcard exemptions in Schedule C and not to any future appreciation in value, the U.S. Court of Appeals for the Third Circuit decides. **Page 1005**

THE TOOLBOX: Some Basic Concepts Under the Bankruptcy Code, Rules
In his monthly column, Judge D. Michael Lynn of the U.S. Bankruptcy Court for the Northern District of Texas discusses concepts that he looks to to inform his interpretation of the Bankruptcy Code and Rules. These concepts include transparency, creditor participation, protection of the status quo ante, fair value to the estate, equitable distribution and the debtor's fresh start. **Page 993**

'Stub Rent' Is Administrative Claim Not Prepetition Unsecured Claim
The rent for the days after the debtor filed its Chapter 11 petition until the next lease payment is due is an administrative claim under Section 365(d)(3) in a prorated amount of a full monthly lease payment, the U.S. Bankruptcy Court for the Central District of California concludes. **Page 997**

Trustee Seeks to Avoid Transfers; Argues Debtor Financed Own Acquisition
The U.S. Bankruptcy Court for the District of Maryland denies in full a motion to dismiss an adversary proceeding in which a Chapter 7 trustee sought to avoid certain transfers made in connection with a leveraged buyout. **Page 999**

5th Cir.: Widow's, Estate's Tax Liabilities Not Excepted From Discharge
The widow of a personal injury lawyer is responsible for $2.7 million in liabilities, the U.S. Court of Appeals for the Fifth Circuit holds, finding that the district court did not err when it concluded that the tax liabilities were excepted from the bankruptcy court's discharge order. **Page 1006**

Indian Tribe and 'Subsidiary' Are Protected by Sovereign Immunity
A bankruptcy court correctly ruled that in enacting Section 106, Congress did not unequivocally express its intent by enacting legislation explicitly abrogating the sovereign immunity of The Lower Sioux Indian Community Tribe and its subsidiary Dakota Finance Corporation, the U.S. Bankruptcy Appellate Panel for the Eighth Circuit decides. **Page 1007**

ALSO IN THE NEWS

APPEALS: The U.S. District Court for the District of Maryland dismisses a debtor's appeal in an adversary proceeding due to his failure to file a timely brief pursuant to Fed.R.Bankr.P. 8009(a). **Page 1008**

MUNICIPALITY: San Bernardino, Calif.'s City Council unanimously votes to approve a fiscal emergency operating plan that will include deferment of general fund debt and lease payments. **Page 1000**

LAW FIRMS: A federal bankruptcy judge will hear in September some of the arguments in a summary judgment motion in Heller Ehrman LLP's fight with law firms where former Heller attorneys and unfinished business landed. **Page 1000**

AIRLINES: Negotiators for the Association of Flight Attendants and bankrupt American Eagle, the regional carrier of American Airlines, reach a tentative labor agreement that would not cut pay or freeze wages. **Page 1001**

ARTICLE SUBMISSIONS

BNA's Bankruptcy Law Reporter invites readers to submit for publication articles of interest to bankruptcy professionals by contacting the managing editor at jhorowitz@bna.com.

Figure 4.1   BNA's Bankruptcy Law Reporter
[Reproduced with permission from BNA's
Bankruptcy Law Reporter, 24 BBLR 989 (Aug. 2, 2012).
Copyright 2012 by The Bureau of National Affairs, Inc.
(800-372-1033) www.bna.com]

electronic formats. Reports on electronic signa-
tures, information licensing, Internet domain
name administration, network security, privacy,
database protection and more. Available on web.
OCLC 34536762
ISSN 1088-5190
LC# 96-642247

Newsletter issues are often routed among the law firm attorneys
or the law school faculty who specialize in those areas. When the
issues are returned to the library, a staff member files them
chronologically in a binder. Each title also has a cumulative index,
updated several times a year. Newsletter routing lists are often a
function of the firm's internal politics. Naturally, partners are listed
before associates, but which partners should come before which
other partners? Sometimes, a partner would ask me to move him
or her up the list, which always put me in an awkward spot, especially when a leapfrogged partner would notice the change and ask
me to change it back. One female partner asked me to put her first
on the list because "the guys all read it in the bathroom, and I don't
want to handle it after them." Some libraries subscribe to multiple
copies of the same newsletter, each with a different routing list, to
avoid these power plays.

I often skimmed newsletters as I was checking them in. This is a
great way to get familiar with the terms, concepts, and concerns in
different areas of law (also true of looseleaf filing), which helped
me provide better reference service. My favorite newsletter? BNA's
Employment Discrimination Report. The idiotic behavior of some
employees—and employers—was fascinating.

Endnotes

1. The nickname refers to South Carolina's official state tree, the Sabal
    Palmetto. See www.netstate.com/states/intro/sc_intro.htm. One of

my library school professors claimed the state was named for the palmetto bug, a species of cockroach. It was gullible of me to believe him; it was idiotic of me to believe him for years.

2. "Using Looseleaf Services," Georgetown Law Library, accessed November 20, 2012, www.ll.georgetown.edu/guides/lls.cfm.

3. Elyse H. Fox, *How to File Looseleaf Services: A Filing Manual and Reference Handbook* (Chapel Hill, NC: Legal Information Services, 2004), 12–13.

4. According to urban legend, in the days before databases like Westlaw and LexisNexis, overzealous law school students would remove pages from looseleafs—or rip them out of case reporters—in the library. Why? To keep other students from reading them, thus giving the vandals a perceived advantage in class discussions. In law firm libraries, pages sometimes go missing, though not to feed insecurities. Instead, it is because an attorney didn't want to carry the whole volume to her office.

5. Fox, 39.

6. Adapted from Fox, 38.

7. Amanda M. Runyon, "The Effect of Economics and Electronic Resources on the Traditional Law Library Print Collection," *Law Library Journal* 101, no. 2 (2009): 189.

8. See Judi, "End of Looseleaf Services?", University of Otago, Law Library Blog, September 21, 2010 (11:40 AM), accessed November 20, 2012, www.otagolawlibrary.blogspot.com/2010/09/end-of-looseleaf-services.html; Ruth Bird, "The Death of the Looseleaf?," Slaw (blog), September 20, 2010, accessed November 20, 2012, www.slaw.ca/2010/09/20/the-death-of-the-looseleaf; Joe Hodnicki, "The Shed West Era in Execution," Law Librarian Blog, June 29, 2010, accessed November 20, 2012, www.lawprofessors.typepad.com/law_librarian_blog/state_county_bar_libraries/page/2.

9. Tredwell, July 15, 2010.

10. Joe Hodnicki, "On Punching Holes: If So-Called 'Loose-leaf' Services are a Pain in the Ass According to TR Legal, What About Pocket-Part Supplemented Titles?," Law Librarian Blog, September 3, 2010, accessed November 20, 2012, www.lawprofessors.typepad.com/law_librarian_blog/2010/09/on-punching-holes-if-so-called-loose-leaf-services-are-a-pain-in-the-ass-according-to-tr-legal-what-.html.

11. Ibid.

12. Ibid.

Chapter 5

The Big Two: Westlaw and LexisNexis

As a law librarian, you will use either Westlaw or LexisNexis, the Big Two of legal databases, for probably 75–80 percent of your research questions. Thus, you need to be an expert on these systems. This chapter is not an extensive course of study on using these databases. Instead, it offers an introduction, a discussion of similarities and differences, advice on when to use them (and when to rely on books), and some details on Westlaw and LexisNexis contracts.

Background

LexisNexis is the older product. It traces its roots to 1968, when the Mead Corporation, a paper manufacturer, bought a smaller company called Data Corporation, creating Mead Data Central. Mead originally purchased the company because it wanted an inkjet printing system developed by Data. After the merger, however, it saw what else Data had been working on: an information retrieval system for the United States Air Force.

This system had also been used to index judicial opinions for the Ohio State Bar, which could now be retrieved by a full-text search. Mead Data named this opinions database LEXIS, and on April 2, 1973, it was offered to attorneys as a way to revolutionize legal research. At first, LEXIS contained only Ohio and New York opinions, but by 1980, it had all U.S. federal and state cases. The same year, Mead Data released NEXIS, a collection of news articles, later combining it with LEXIS to form LEXIS-NEXIS.[1]

Naturally, West Publishing was very interested in the development of LEXIS, particularly in the rates charged to attorneys to connect to the Mead Central mainframe. The president of West, Dwight Opperman, thought his company could provide a better service. After all, West had been publishing case law for nearly a hundred years, and its summaries and indexing (i.e., the topic and key number system) would provide significant enhancements over LEXIS. Thus, in 1975, Westlaw was born.[2]

It didn't take the two companies long to start a feud. In 1985, Lexis, which had always put the West reporter citation on the first screen of its digitized cases, announced it would put West page numbers throughout each case, enabling LexisNexis users to pinpoint (i.e., cite to a page number within the case) without consulting a print reporter. West sued Lexis, claiming its plan was "an appropriation of West's comprehensive arrangement of case reports in violation of the Copyright Act of 1976," and won the suit.[3] Lexis agreed to pay $50,000 a year to license West's pagination and text corrections, an agreement voided by a later case in which the Second Circuit ruled that West's page numbering and other enhancements were "obvious, typical, and lacking even minimal creativity."[4] In other words, they were not copyrightable.[5]

These days, Westlaw and LexisNexis are the Ford and Chevrolet of legal research databases (others will be discussed in Chapter 6). Each has some unique content and superior features; I'll discuss these differences later in the chapter.

Print vs. Electronic

First, however, understand this: Print vs. electronic research is the biggest battle you'll fight as a librarian. People will ask you all the time why you have all these books when "everything is online." It's a good question. You need a good answer, and not just to keep your library from being turned into a computer lab. As a librarian, your job is to help people find the right information quickly and inexpensively. Wexis[6] and other databases will work a lot of the time, but not always. When should you use which?

When to Use Print Sources

There are several good reasons to turn to print sources:[7]

- You need background information on an unfamiliar area of law.

- You are researching complex concepts or legal theories. Print is quicker and cheaper than pay-per-view databases.

- Your research involves commonplace terms, ambiguous words, or words with many synonyms. This kind of research is better done with a topical index than a keyword search.

- Your area of law is more commonly known by a slang term such as *lemon law*. Most people know this term, and most states have a lemon law statute, but the statute may not include the phrase *lemon law*. North Carolina's does not, though the index to the statutes does have a *lemon law* heading.

- You need historical materials, which are more likely to be found in print.

- An initial online search has given you too much or too little information.

When to Use Electronic Sources

There are also good reasons to use electronic resources:

- You want to retrieve a document by citation.

- You need a case using an exact phrase (see Chapter 9 for an example).

- You are researching a new area of law (e.g., social networking sites).

- You need a cross-jurisdictional search. It is easier to search one database of all 50 states' case law than to look up the same topic and key number in every West digest.

- You need to refer to an unpublished case. These are easier to find online.

What Westlaw and LexisNexis Have in Common

Westlaw and LexisNexis both contain the following:

- All U.S. and state case law ever published (and lots of unpublished cases[8])

- All current U.S. and state statutes (older statutes go back about 10 years, though this varies by state)

- U.S. and state legislative history documents back to the mid-1990s, though this coverage varies by state

- Select U.S. and state court filings

- Thousands of newspaper, magazine, and scholarly articles from both law and nonlaw periodicals (titles differ by provider[9])

- Full-text treatises (titles differ by provider)

- Public and private U.S. company data, including earnings, mergers, acquisitions, bankruptcies, executive profiles, and brokerage research (sources differ by provider)

- Public records, including voter registrations, death records, assets (cars, boats, planes, real property), licenses (driver, professional, pilot, hunting, and fishing), and business records (UCC, FEIN, Dun & Bradstreet)

- Select case law and statutes from other countries (sources differ by provider)

Westlaw Basics

Since it began in 1975, Westlaw has undergone many changes. The most comprehensive of these was WestlawNext, which was released in 2010. You can find online training programs and detailed user guides for Westlaw and WestlawNext at www.store.westlaw.com. Here, I provide the basics of WestlawNext. To start, go to www.next.westlaw.com and sign in.

To perform research for a specific law firm client, enter your firm's client ID number. This will show up on your Westlaw invoice for easy client bill-back. Next, choose how the firm should be billed for the research: hourly (i.e., per minute spent online) or transactional (i.e., per search or document retrieved). My advice is to choose hourly if you plan to do a lot of quick searches and print or email the results, or if you are going to search expensive databases (e.g., public records). Choose transactional if you plan on just a few searches, or prefer to read documents online. Then click Continue. This brings you to the main menu (Figure 5.1).

From this menu, select the type of material you want—cases, statutes, secondary sources, forms, whatever. Drill down through the subsequent menus until you come to a search box. You will know what to do from there.

One important feature of Westlaw is the topic and key number system, West's unique contribution to American jurisprudence. This information was available on the old Westlaw interface but was hard to find and cumbersome to use. To find it on WestlawNext, simply click Tools, then West Key Number System (Figure 5.2).

ⅲ Browse				
All Content	Federal Materials	State Materials	Topics	Tools

Cases	Briefs	Dockets
Statutes & Court Rules	Trial Court Documents	News
Regulations	Expert Materials	Patents
Administrative Decisions & Guidance	Jury Verdicts & Settlements	Public Records ⬀
Trial Court Orders	Proposed & Enacted Legislation	Trial & Oral Argument Transcripts
Secondary Sources		Directories
Forms	Proposed & Adopted Regulations	Business Information
		International Materials

Figure 5.1   WestlawNext main search screen

Click the topic you want, for example Parent and Child (Figure 5.3). Select the subtopic or key number (e.g., ☛ 4 Support of parent by child). Then you can change jurisdiction, save or email your results, or click any of the case links. Figure 5.4 shows the first two cases, *Herbst v. Krause* and *Kruithof v. Hartford Acc. & Indem. Co.*

Instead of using the menus, of course, you could start with the search box, the biggest innovation of WestlawNext. Their new search box was modeled after Google's, and you can enter anything into it—keywords, citations, whatever—to get your results. This is a major change from the old Westlaw interface, where you had to drill down through menus to select an individual database before searching. Now you can do what Google has taught us: Just type and click.

The ease of this one-stop search box, however, obscures an important potential cost-saving strategy: The larger the database, the more expensive it is to search.[10] A database that includes all federal and state cases, for example, costs more per search than a database with just state cases, which in turn is more costly than the one limited to North Carolina cases. If you know you need a North

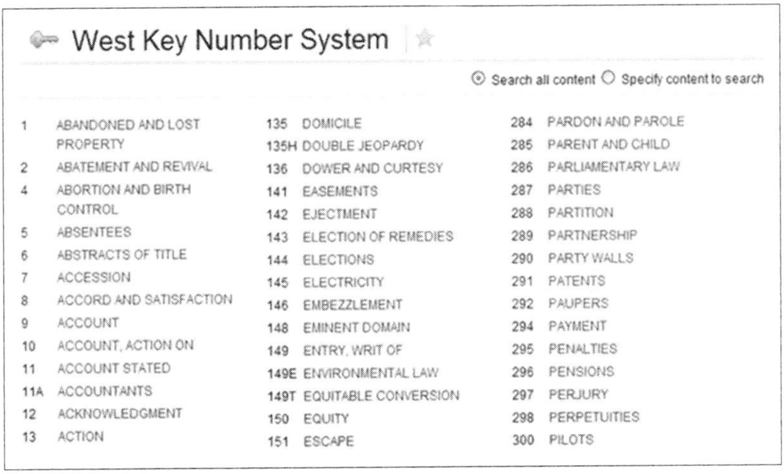

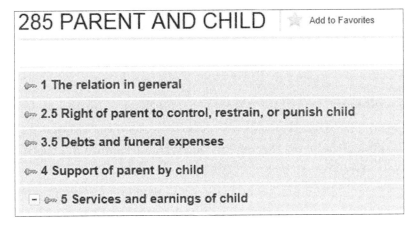

Figure 5.2   West key number system

285 PARENT AND CHILD ☆ Add to Favorites

⚷ **1 The relation in general**

⚷ **2.5 Right of parent to control, restrain, or punish child**

⚷ **3.5 Debts and funeral expenses**

⚷ **4 Support of parent by child**

[–] ⚷ **5 Services and earnings of child**

Figure 5.3   Choosing your topic

Carolina case, then there is no point in searching an all-case database. Searching the smallest database that contains your needed content incurs the smallest charge. You can choose your jurisdiction, which chooses your database, using the drop-down menu next to the search box, but this path allows less control than the old Westlaw menu. Besides, it isn't the Google way of type-and-click.

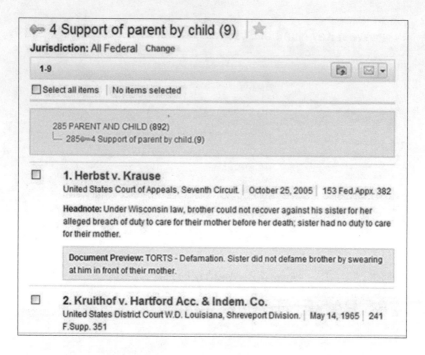

Figure 5.4   First two cases in your search results

Suppose I search for *alienation of affection* in North Carolina cases. I get a list of entries with case name, date and citation, and a summary with my search terms highlighted. Figure 5.5 shows the first of these cases, *Pharr v. Beck.*

To the left of the list of cases is ResultsPlus (a feature before WestlawNext), which links directly to any statutes, administrative regs or rulings, secondary sources, or other documents on the same topic (Figure 5.6). Use these with care: Each click results in a separate charge.

Back to *Pharr v. Beck.* Do you see the red flag beside the name in Figure 5.5? This flag is the KeyCite symbol. KeyCite is an electronic citator, a tool used to determine whether a case is still "good law" (see Chapter 2). You can choose KeyCite from the Tools menu or, in the search box, type *keycite* before a citation. This gives you a list of

☐ ⚑ **Pharr v. Beck**
Court of Appeals of North Carolina. | November 20, 2001 | 147 N.C.App. 268

FAMILY LAW - Marriage. Evidence supported finding that other woman's conduct caused husband's loss of **affection** for wife.

...A claim for **alienation** of **affection** requires proof of three elements: (1) there was a marriage with love and **affection** existing between the husband and wife; (2) that love and **affection** was **alienated**, which occurs if a spouse's **affection** for the other spouse is destroyed or diminished; and (3) the malicious acts of the defendant produced the loss of that love and **affection**...

...[1] A claim for **alienation** of **affection** requires proof of three elements: (1) there was a marriage with love and **affection** existing between the husband and wife; (2) that love and **affection** was **alienated**; 1 and (3) the malicious acts of the defendant produced the loss of that love and **affection**...

Figure 5.5   Pharr v. Beck alienation of affection case

Overview	14
Cases	129
Statutes	59
Regulations	5
Administrative Decisions & Guidance	18
Trial Court Orders	33
Secondary Sources	1,936
Forms	37
Briefs	118
Trial Court Documents	56
Expert Materials	4
Jury Verdicts & Settlements	101
Proposed & Enacted Legislation	36
Proposed & Adopted Regulations	6
All Results	2,538

Figure 5.6   ResultsPlus

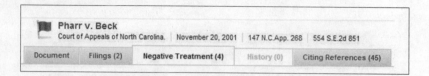

Figure 5.7   List organized into tabs

cases, statutes, and secondary sources that have cited your case. The list is organized into tabs, as shown in Figure 5.7.

Looking at these tabs, I quickly see that four other cases have treated *Pharr* negatively, either by rejecting its reasoning or directly overruling it as in *McCutchen v. McCutchen*, 360 N.C. 280, 624 S.E.2d 620 (N.C. 2006). Because *Pharr*, a North Carolina Court of Appeals case, was overruled by *McCutchen*, a North Carolina Supreme Court case, subsequent North Carolina judges can no longer rely on the reasoning in *Pharr* to support their rulings. This is what attorneys mean when they say a case is no longer "good law."

On WestlawNext, secondary sources are where you can really rack up charges, so for them, I don't suggest using the all-purpose search box. Suppose I want to research the term *Panduit kicker*. I could type this into the search box and get hundreds of hits. A more cost-effective approach, however, would be first to use Google to get a rough definition of the term: "The concept of the Panduit kicker, or infringement kicker, originated with *Panduit Corporation v. Stahlin Bros. Fibre Works, Inc.*"[11]

Now I know enough to choose a specific treatise. From the main menu, I select Secondary Sources, then Intellectual Property, then Texts & Treatises, where I see a title called *Calculating Intellectual Property Damages*. This is consistent with what I read in the Google source. Clicking on this link, I can browse the treatise table of contents or access a digital version of the book index. From there, I can easily find *Panduit kicker* in the P section. If I had already known I wanted *Calculating Intellectual Property Damages*, I could have gone to the main menu, clicked on

Secondary Sources, and then chosen the title from the Secondary Sources Index, an alphabetical list of all treatises and journals on Westlaw.

LexisNexis Basics

LexisNexis also has a new version: Lexis Advance, which differs from old LexisNexis in the same way WestlawNext differs from old Westlaw. The following list shows how LexisNexis compares to Westlaw in a few key areas:

- LexisNexis includes Martindale-Hubbell, the world's leading law firm directory.

- LexisNexis incorporates *Shepard's*, the older and more respected citator.

- Each provides different treatises and news sources. LexisNexis has business news and information from the Dow Jones Factiva database, with the biggest source being the *Wall Street Journal*; Westlaw has only the *Wall Street Journal*'s abstracts).[12]

- The West topic and key number system is not used in LexisNexis, which was forced to develop its own case law indexing system. I find that no one uses the LexisNexis indexing system.

- Searchers do use LexisNexis SmartIndexing, a classification system of online tags, for news articles and corporate documents. At least, I have.[13]

LexisNexis tutorials and user guides are available at support. lexisnexis.com. The basics are as follows.

To start, go to www.advance.lexis.com and sign in. As with WestlawNext, you are greeted with a Google-like search box on the homepage. Three tabs under the search box let you browse or limit your search by content type (case, statute, treatise, regulation), jurisdiction (U.S., all states, individual states), or practice area (contracts, labor and employment, copyright, environmental).

Suppose I want to find a copyright case involving the reclusive American author J. D. Salinger. In the search box, I create a search as shown in Figure 5.8 and get over 36,000 hits—too many to contemplate.

Next I try a Boolean AND search, as shown in Figure 5.9. This cuts the results to 185, and I immediately see a major difference from the old LexisNexis search function. If you enter two terms in Lexis Advance with no connector, the default is an OR search. (With the old LexisNexis, the default was an AND search.)

Could I whittle the results even more? You bet. In the search shown in Figure 5.10, /s is used to guarantee the results have *salinger* within the same sentence as *copyright*.

Now I get 85 results, a manageable number, though I notice only a few are cases *involving* J. D. Salinger. Most are cases *citing* one of

Figure 5.8   Search leading to excessive search results

Figure 5.9   Default OR search

Figure 5.10   Using /s to refine results

the Salinger cases. Can I write a search that returns only cases where Salinger is a party?

As far as I can tell, no, which is unfortunate. Using the old LexisNexis, when I typed *NAME(salinger) and copyright*, I got only those cases with Salinger in the name—*Salinger v. Colting*, 607 F.3d 68 (2d Cir., 2010) and *Salinger v. Random House*, 818 F.2d 252 (2d Cir., 1987), for example. Furthermore, I was able to restrict a search by court name, judge's name, attorneys' names, date, or two dozen other factors. These controls seem lost in Lexis Advance, though some of them remain in WestlawNext (where, for example, when I enter *title(salinger) and copyright*, I get only the cases with Salinger in the title[14]).

This is more than an annoyance; it is a concession to users' eroding search skills. LexisNexis and Westlaw have made their new interfaces look like Google to appeal to 20-somethings who grew up with the search giant. By apparently discarding a whole category of search restrictions useful to a savvy researcher, Lexis Advance now functions more like Google: Just type and click. With a simplified search process, however, precision is lost. Instead of running the narrowest search in the smallest database to return the least results, searchers will do quick, broad, Google-type searches, then spend their time clicking on results.

This approach benefits West and Lexis more than the users. By adding to the time spent online as well as the number of clicks, the companies are stoking their revenue. Firms will end up paying more for database use, which means they pass along more expenses to their clients. Clients could also pay more in billable hours as attorneys spend more time picking through big bouquets of results. This type of search could also prompt attorneys to make do with the first results they see, which may not be the best results. My advice, therefore, is to use WestlawNext and Lexis Advance with caution.

Just as Westlaw has KeyCite to determine whether a case is "good law," LexisNexis has *Shepard's*. Attorneys will often ask you to Shepardize a case, meaning they want to know how that case has been treated by subsequent courts. Instead of red and yellow flags, *Shepard's* uses various symbols. (Figure 2.1 on page 29 provides an illustration of the KeyCite and *Shepard's* symbols.)

Let's consider *Pharr v. Beck* again. Type *shep: 147 nc app 268* in the search box. The results show 10 cases and 12 secondary sources citing *Pharr* (Figure 5.11). See the red octagon? It lets you know *Pharr* has been overturned, just as the red flag did in KeyCite.

Table 5.1[15] provides a more extensive comparison of features in *Shepard's* and KeyCite.

Contracts

In 2001, the law department at Duke Energy Corporation, where I was the library director, spent about $360,000 on LexisNexis. Duke Energy at that time was the 14th-largest U.S. company. Less than a decade later, the 200 largest U.S. law firms were spending an average of $1.4 million a year on LexisNexis and $1.6 million on Westlaw.[16] Solo practitioners, on the other hand, can pay as little as $180 a month.[17] Public libraries tend to pay a little more, usually a few thousand per year.

What accounts for these price variations? Mainly, these stem from differences in content and user base. Small firms have few users, maybe just one or two. Moreover, they practice in a handful of areas and jurisdictions, meaning they need just a fraction of what's available on Westlaw or LexisNexis. By contrast, Baker &

Pharr v. Beck, 14... ✕

Appellate History (1) | **Citing Decisions (10)** | Citing Law Reviews, Treatises... (12)

Shepard's®: ● Pharr v. Beck, 147 N.C. App. 268, 554 S.E.2d 851, 2001 N.C. App. LEXIS 1144 (N.C. Ct. App. 2001)

Figure 5.11 Shepardizing a case

Table 5.1   Comparing Features in *Shepard's* and KeyCite.

	Shepard's	KeyCite
Signals		
Negative treatment: Case is not good law for at least one of its points (overruled or reversed); statute has been amended or repealed.	Red stop sign	Red flag
Questioned by: Citing opinions question continuing validity or precedential value of case because of intervening circumstances, including judicial or legislative overruling.	Orange "Q"	N/A
Caution: Case has some negative history (limited, criticized); statute has section affected by pending legislation.	Yellow triangle	Yellow flag
Positive treatment: History or treatment of case has positive impact on your case (affirmed, followed).	Green diamond with "+"	N/A
Case has some **analysis**, which is neither positive nor negative.	"A" in blue circle	N/A
Case has some **history**.	"A" in blue circle	Blue "H"
Case is cited, with **no analysis**.	"I" in blue circle	Green "C"
Results may be marked as follows		
Editorial treatment, editorial analysis	- Followed, criticized, distinguished, harmonized, explained, etc. - Identifies at a glance whether a case is overruled for one point of law, but followed on another, as well as if one jurisdiction followed but another overruled. KeyCite does not uncover these splits of authority at a glance.	- Distinguished by, declined to extend, disagreement recognized by, examined by, discussed by, cited by, mentioned by
Citing case or decision directly quotes cited case	- N/A	- Quotation marks appear after the cite.
Indicates which headnotes from the case in question are discussed in the subsequent case	- Headnotes are indicated after the cite.	- Headnotes are indicated after the cite.
Depth of treatment of cited case	- Very negative treatment (e.g., overruled), validity questioned (e.g., questioned by), mild negative (e.g., criticized), neutral (e.g., explained), to the positive (e.g., followed by)	- One to four stars, from mentioned to extended examination. The stars indicate how *long* the case talked about the case in question. Cases with one star may have relied heavily on the case, but did not go on at length.
Search features and other functions		
Table of authorities (TOA) in cited case	- Includes TOA, with editorial treatment to indicate how the case in question treated the cases it cited to. - Lexis Advance uses Trail of Authorities in place of TOA. Click on Activate Passages, and squares will appear around the issues in the case. Click in the issue box for a list of subsequent cases dealing with that issue.	- No TOA (no editorial treatment) in old Westlaw. - WestlawNext does not have TOA.

Table 5.1 (cont.)

To search within results	- Lexis Advance has Narrow by Options in the left bar.	- WestlawNext uses Narrow by Filters.
Limiting the results	- By editorial analysis (distinguished, followed, cited by etc.), focus (search for terms in the cases), date, jurisdiction, LexisNexis headnotes and Westlaw headnotes. Can also limit by positive or negative treatment and type of document using the summary table at the beginning of the Shepard's report. - LexisNexis results are already arranged by jurisdiction. - Lexis Advance can limit by editorial analysis (distinguished, followed, cited by etc.), jurisdiction, LexisNexis headnote, search terms, date.	- Westlaw headnotes, locate (search for terms in the cases), jurisdiction, date, depth of treatment and document type. Filtering options are on separate pages. - WestlawNext has all filtering available from the left bar. There is an additional filter for reported v. unreported.
Graphical chart of citing cases	- Lexis Advance has a Citing Decisions Grid showing a graphical representation of the citing cases. - Shepard's graphical also shows subsequent citing cases to indicate where the case stands today.	- N/A
Graphical history	- Lexis Advance has a map, Shepard's graphical, showing subsequent appellate history, both in the case itself and subsequent citing cases.	- Yes, similar to Lexis Advance

McKenzie, the nation's biggest law firm, has almost 3,800 attorneys and had an income of $2.27 billion in 2011.[18] A firm that size can afford full access to both providers. Most public libraries have even larger user bases, but the users are not high-stakes negotiators handling seven-figure deals. They are average people with average needs—say, a do-it-yourself divorce. Such needs do not justify top-dollar access.

Because they serve an ever-changing population, public libraries with Westlaw or LexisNexis have flat-rate contracts, providing unlimited access to select databases (see, for example, Westlaw Patron Access, discussed in Chapter 1). The more databases selected, the more the library pays. Law firms can also negotiate flat-rate contracts, giving unlimited access to their 500-plus or 1,000-plus or 3,000-plus attorneys (not to mention all the paralegals, librarians, and other support staff). These contracts discount the regular database rates. Thus, even though a firm's monthly invoice will show, say, $500,000 in usage, the actual cost will be discounted to the flat-rate amount, which might be only $100,000. This makes budgeting easier for the firm and guarantees the vendor a certain steady level of revenue.

These types of contracts, however, make it trickier for a law firm to charge the cost to clients. Recall that Westlaw and LexisNexis allow you to enter a client ID number at the start of each research session. Each vendor breaks down its monthly invoice by client ID, making it easy to add these charges to client bills. Some firms include these exact costs on client bills—even though the costs, thanks to the flat-rate discount, are not what the firm actually pays. Other firms calculate their discount, and pass it along to their clients.

Increasingly, however, big corporate clients are refusing to pay for research costs, a change that the law firms, unwilling to lose those clients, can't fight.[19] If that $100,000 is *all* overhead, then the firms have an incentive to be cost-effective. Why? Because each year's contract is based on the past year's usage. The flat rate is an estimate, and if the firm exceeds the estimate according to its actual invoices, then next year's rate might be higher. Also, some Westlaw and LexisNexis databases cannot be offered under a flat rate (public records, for example, or content licensed from Bureau of National Affairs, Common Clearing House, or rival legal publishers). These searches are billed at the regular price, so it is crucial to understand the techniques of cost-effective searching for these databases.

Attorneys, however, don't really understand this. (At least, the ones I worked with didn't.) For instance, attorneys would tell summer interns not to use Westlaw or LexisNexis, fearing their inexperience would run up a huge bill for a client. The interns would mope around the library, doubtful of the books, until I explained to the supervising attorney that they could search all day without costing us an extra cent. (West and Lexis expect interns to be inefficient, so they ignore the interns' research costs.) They were always delighted to hear this, and I hoped each time that they would rush back to the firm management committee, repeat the tidings, and usher in a period of PaxChargebacka. Alas, none of them ever did.

In the early days of electronic legal research, no one worried about cost. One blogger reminisces about those days before lamenting that they are over:

> When I left library school for a mid-sized Chicago SEC law firm in 1980 I thought I arrived in legal research heaven. Don't worry about Lexis costs for research. Go ahead and use Dow Jones online to get the latest headline news on a hostile takeover. Have a court clerk express mail the pleading just filed. Ditto for an SEC filing from Charlie Simon's information brokerage in D.C. Time really was of the essence and the client was billed the cost of research and document retrieval. My colleagues in academic law libraries turned around research projects over the course of several days and even weeks. Law firm librarians turned around similar research assignments overnight or in 48 hours. They had information at their finger tips [in] as close to real time as was possible back [then] because of law firm cost recovery practices. And clients paid. The costs were deducted as business expenses.[20]

Big corporate clients now assert greater control over law firm billing, refusing, in some cases, to cover Westlaw or LexisNexis research costs. Your expertise on these systems, both as a user and a contract administrator, is one of the most valuable skills you can develop as a law librarian.

Which Is Better?

Were you thinking this question as you read this chapter? If so, good; you will hear it a lot from your patrons. Several websites compare Westlaw and LexisNexis (see, for example, www.law.csuohio. edu/lawlibrary/guides/wexisnextcompared), and in 2008, more than 700 law librarians answered a Stanford University survey on the topic.[21] My answer? You need both. Some people say that the main value of having both is to play the vendors off each other. When it's time to renegotiate your Westlaw contract, for instance, tell the West folks about your LexisNexis contract and get them to sweeten the deal.

To me, this is a wrong-headed strategy. The advantages of having both systems outweigh any possible benefit from a price war. Westlaw has better treatises; LexisNexis has better journals. Westlaw has more medical information; LexisNexis has more corporate and business documents. Westlaw has the *National Reporter System*; LexisNexis has *Shepard's*. Full-service law firms usually subscribe to both, so to be a full-service law librarian, you need to be an expert in both. Neither one is going anywhere despite the rise of low-cost alternatives and other competitors, a topic I will take up in Chapter 6.

Endnotes

1. In the 1990s, LEXIS-NEXIS was lowercased to Lexis-Nexis. The official spelling is now sans hyphen: LexisNexis. A rite of passage for law librarians is explaining to some lawyer, administrator, or board member that the product is *not* spelled Lexus-Nexus. The confusion is understandable, I guess, when you consider the type of vehicle that attorneys usually drive.
2. Erin Carlyle, "Westlaw Rises to Legal Publishing Fame by Selling Free Information," Citypages, April 29, 2009, accessed November 21, 2012, www.citypages.com/2009-04-29/news/westlaw-rises-to-legal-publishing-fame-by-selling-free-information.
3. *West Pub. Co. v. Mead Data Cent., Inc.*, 799 F. 2d 1219 (8thCir., 1986).

4. *Matthew Bender & Co., Inc. v. West Pub. Co.*, 158 F. 3d 674 (2ndCir., 1998).

5. For more on these cases, see Ann Jennings, "The West Copyright Conundrum," in *Publishing and the Law: Current Legal Issues*, A. Bruce Strauch, ed. (New York: Haworth, 2001), 109–125.

6. Westlaw and LexisNexis, considered collectively. It is the librarian equivalent of Brangelina and Bennifer.

7. This section and the next adapted from Virginia Tucker and Marc Lampson, *Finding the Answers to Legal Questions: A How-To-Do-It Manual* (New York: Neal-Schuman, 2011).

8. Unpublished judicial opinions are opinions not selected for inclusion in the *National Reporter System*. They are useful as windows into how the court rules on particular issues, but they generally do *not* have precedential value. In other words, they cannot be cited in court documents.

9. These are text only—no tables, charts, graphs, or pictures. I've had attorneys ask me for an article because they wanted the illustration, not the text. I had to find such articles through means other than Wexis.

10. This is just one of several tips for cost-effective Westlaw use. For others, see www.tinyurl.com/7haxl6v. LexisNexis tips are available at www.tinyurl.com/7ewaed2.

11. Gordon V. Smith and Russell L. Parr, *Intellectual Property: Valuation, Exploitation, and Infringement Damages*, 4th ed. (Hoboken, NJ: John Wiley & Sons, 2005).

12. To see any of the 50,000-plus LexisNexis sources, go to w3.nexis.com/sources.

13. For details, see law.lexisnexis.com/infopro/Training-and-Resources/SmartIndexing-Resource-Center.

14. For details on LexisNexis terms and connectors, see www.snipurl.com/2289cr0. For details on Westlaw terms and connectors, see www.snipurl.com/26otht7.

15. Adapted from Cleveland-Marshall College of Law Library, www.law.csuohio.edu/lawlibrary/guides/shepardskeycite.

16. "Law Librarian Survey," *American Lawyer*, July 1, 2011, accessed November 21, 2012, www.snipurl.com/228alje.

17. Robert J. Ambrogi, "What Do You Pay for Westlaw or LexisNexis?" Robert Ambrogi's LawSites (blog), July 13, 2011, accessed November 21, 2012, www.lawsitesblog.com/2011/07/what-do-you-pay-for-westlaw-or-lexisnexis.html.

18. Drew Combs, "At Baker & McKenzie, Profits and Revenues up in 2011," AmLaw Daily, August 17, 2011, accessed November 21, 2012, www.amlawdaily.typepad.com/amlawdaily/2011/08/at-baker-mckenzie-profits-and-revnues-up-for-fy2011.html.

19. See "Legal Research One of Leading Irritants says New Survey on Cost Recovery," Strategic Librarian (blog), April 22, 2011, accessed November 21, 2012, www.strategiclibrarian.com/2011/04/22/legal-research-one-of-leading-irritants-says-new-survey-on-cost-recovery.

20. Joe Hodnicki, "The Future of Westlaw and LexisNexis Pricing or How the 'Radical Transformation of the Legal Publishing Marketplace' May Not Save Law Libraries Much Money," Law Librarian Blog (blog), August 19, 2009, accessed November 21, 2012, www.law professors.typepad.com/law_librarian_blog/2009/08/the-future-of-westlaw-and-lexisnexis-pricing-in-the-radical-transformation-of-the-legal-publishing-m.html.

21. J. Paul Lomio and Erika V. Wayne, "Law Librarians and LexisNexis vs. Westlaw: Survey Results," accessed January 3, 2013, www.law.stanford.edu/sites/default/files/biblio/1002/145874/doc/slspublic/lomio wayne-rp23.pdf.

Chapter 6

Beyond the Big Two: Other Legal Databases

Companies trying to compete with Westlaw and LexisNexis have, according to Greg Lambert, "a huge uphill battle to wage."[1] None of them, he asserts, speaks with the authority of the Big Two, which is a significant fact—perhaps the only fact worth considering. Why?

> [L]et's remember what is the "end game" of legal research. When all is said and done, your final product should be something that is upheld by a court of law. Within the common law courts, this generally means that you must point to existing documents that support your claim. The whole idea behind such concepts as *stare decisis* is that the "law" is built upon existing law and decisions and is usually not changed except in extreme circumstances. When you have concepts like *stare decisis*, you need to be able to rely upon solid resources that have earned the trust of the courts. It may be true that information is liquid, but laws and the legal information behind those laws are much more like ice than they are like water.[2]

In other words, Lambert thinks the cases, statutes, regulations, treatises, journals, and other sources on Wexis are the only sources that a court of law will accept. And isn't that the whole point of legal practice?

West and Lexis don't write cases, statutes, and regulations, however; they just publish them. Other databases, some of them just as sophisticated and user-friendly, also do this. Moreover, West or Lexis treatises are *not* the most respected in some practice areas, including tax and labor law. For tax law, the *ne plus ultra* is Common Clearing House (CCH) or Research Institute of America; for labor law, it's the Bureau of National Affairs (BNA).

Who is the best of the rest? This chapter will divide these resources into three categories: supplemental databases, low-cost alternatives, and free legal websites.

Supplemental Databases

Supplemental databases are niche products that lack the scope of Westlaw and LexisNexis. Instead, they focus on one or two areas of law, often surpassing the Big Two in those specific areas. They are generally cheaper and offer excellent customer support.

HeinOnline

HeinOnline (www.heinonline.org) is run by the William S. Hein Company, which calls its database the world's largest "image-based" legal research database. Unlike the text documents of Westlaw and LexisNexis, all the documents on HeinOnline are PDF images of the original print copies. Wexis is still the place for everyday primary law—cases, statutes, and regs. HeinOnline specializes in lesser-known but harder-to-find materials, including:

- United Nations documents

- Official and unofficial U.S. treaties

- English case law back to 1220

- Unpublished and out-of-print American Law Institute documents

- U.S. legislative histories, Congressional documents, and presidential papers

The most-used content on HeinOnline, however, is the law journals. Westlaw and LexisNexis have journal articles, but they go back only to the early 1980s. HeinOnline's coverage often begins with a journal's *very first issue*, which, for some journals, means reaching back to the 1800s.

Suppose I wanted to read the first article in the inaugural issue, April 15, 1887, of *Harvard Law Review*. After signing on, I select Law Journal Library, and then browse by publication title. I choose H from the list and find *Harvard Law Review*.

Next, I click the + symbol to expand to all 124 volumes, and then expand Volume 1 to see Issue 1, Issue 2, and so on. Finally, I select the first article under Issue 1 (see Figure 6.1).

I could also search for an author, article title, publication title, or keyword across multiple documents. For help on searching, see the HeinOnline training website (home.heinonline.org/resources/help-training/guides).

ProQuest Congressional

Though HeinOnline includes legislative history documents, a better database for this information is ProQuest Congressional, formerly called LexisNexis Congressional. (ProQuest acquired the system from Lexis in 2010.[3]) What is legislative history? At each stage of the law-making process, the legislators create documents—committee reports, committee hearings, bills, amendments, sponsor remarks, expert testimonies, and the like. Attorneys and judges often use such documents to understand *legislative intent*, or why a legislature enacted a particular statute.[4]

Figure 6.2 shows the types of documents available on ProQuest Congressional.

There is no browse feature so you'll need to use the search boxes. If I search the title field for *ufos*, I find *The UFO Enigma*, a 1983 report from the Congressional Research Service. One caveat: For many documents, all you get is an index entry, not the full text.

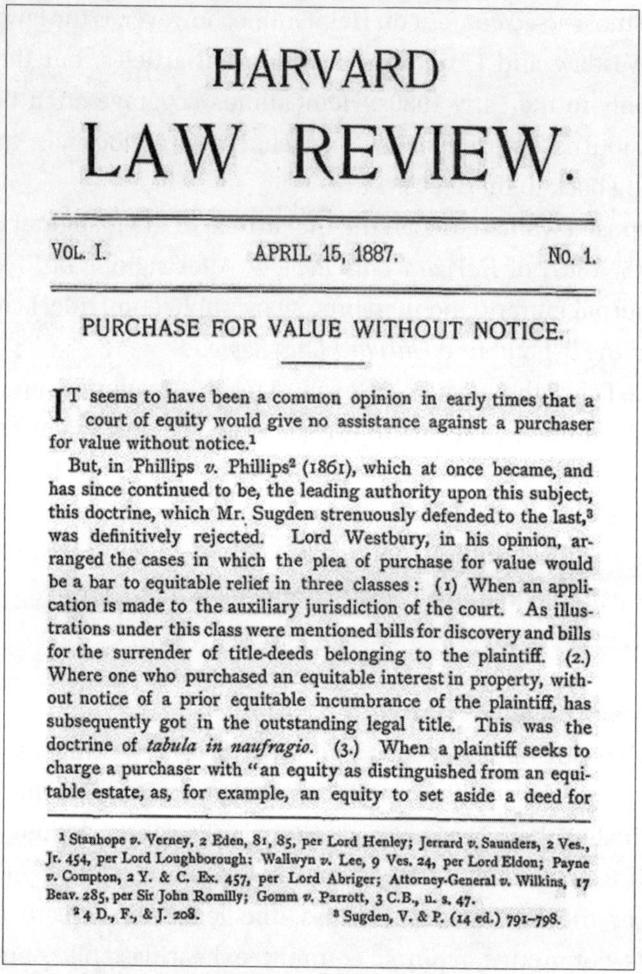

HARVARD

LAW REVIEW.

VOL. I. APRIL 15, 1887. NO. 1.

PURCHASE FOR VALUE WITHOUT NOTICE.

IT seems to have been a common opinion in early times that a court of equity would give no assistance against a purchaser for value without notice.[1]

But, in Phillips *v.* Phillips[2] (1861), which at once became, and has since continued to be, the leading authority upon this subject, this doctrine, which Mr. Sugden strenuously defended to the last,[3] was definitively rejected. Lord Westbury, in his opinion, arranged the cases in which the plea of purchase for value would be a bar to equitable relief in three classes: (1) When an application is made to the auxiliary jurisdiction of the court. As illustrations under this class were mentioned bills for discovery and bills for the surrender of title-deeds belonging to the plaintiff. (2.) Where one who purchased an equitable interest in property, without notice of a prior equitable incumbrance of the plaintiff, has subsequently got in the outstanding legal title. This was the doctrine of *tabula in naufragio*. (3.) When a plaintiff seeks to charge a purchaser with "an equity as distinguished from an equitable estate, as, for example, an equity to set aside a deed for

[1] Stanhope *v.* Verney, 2 Eden, 81, 85, per Lord Henley; Jerrard *v.* Saunders, 2 Ves., Jr. 454, per Lord Loughborough: Wallwyn *v.* Lee, 9 Ves. 24, per Lord Eldon; Payne *v.* Compton, 2 Y. & C. Ex. 457, per Lord Abriger; Attorney-General *v.* Wilkins, 17 Beav. 285, per Sir John Romilly; Gomm *v.* Parrott, 3 C.B., n. s. 47.

[2] 4 D., F., & J. 208.

[3] Sugden, V. & P. (14 ed.) 791–798.

Figure 6.1 The first article of *Harvard Law Review*

However, even this is useful. Legislative history research is confusing, even to experienced attorneys. They may ask for a *committee report* when what they need is a *committee print*—not the same thing. It will be up to you to master the nuances of legislative history. Three excellent starting points are the LLSDC's Legislative

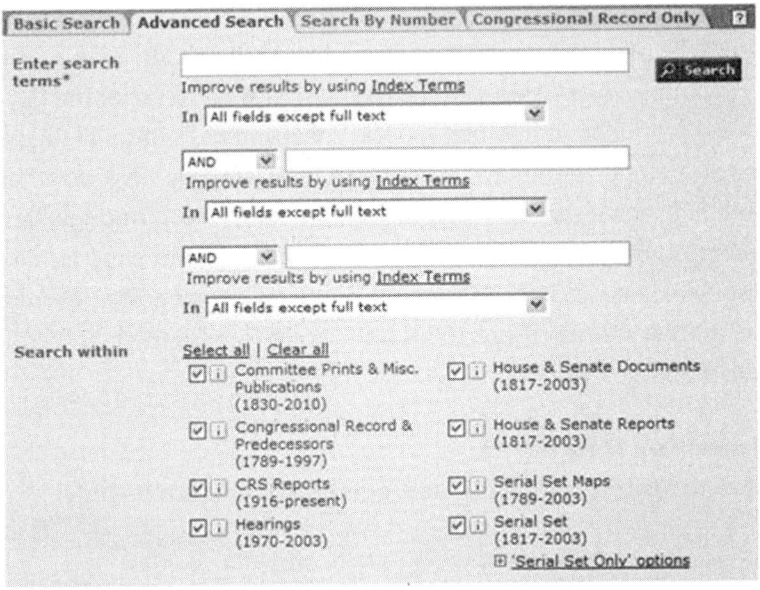

Figure 6.2   Types of documents available on ProQuest Congressional

Source Book (www.llsdc.org/sourcebook), Federal Legislative History (lib.law.washington.edu/ref/fedlegishist.html), and State Legislative History Research Guides on the Web (www.tinyurl.com/3kqveb).

LegalTrac

InfoTrac is a well-known serials database from Gale. Its legal database is called LegalTrac, which indexes more than 1,500 law reviews, legal newspapers, bar association journals, and international legal journals, plus another 1,000 business and general-interest titles. Some articles are full-text; most are not. LegalTrac's real value is as an index.

One thing to note: LegalTrac indexes some journals that are *not* included in Westlaw, LexisNexis, or HeinOnline.

Bloomberg BNA

The BNA (www.bna.com) was started in 1929 as a division of the newspaper *United States Daily*. Its mission was "to cover the day-to-day workings of a young federal government."[5] Initially focusing on patent, trademark, and copyright cases, the BNA now has over 300 news services covering many subjects: corporate law, labor and employment law, the environment, health care, human resources, tax, and accounting. BNA stayed independent through the merger mania of the 1980s and 1990s (see Chapter 1) before succumbing to Bloomberg in 2011.[6]

Other Key Databases

Beyond the few just mentioned, other key databases include:

- CCH IntelliConnect (www.intelliconnect.cch.com): Includes CCH's leading commentaries on tax and labor law.

- IndexMaster (www.indexmaster.com): Collects the index and table of contents of more than 8,000 treatises into one database.

- LLMC-Digital (www.llmc-digital.org): Includes historical and non-U.S materials not found elsewhere.

- RIA Checkpoint (www.checkpoint.riag.com): Rivals CCH in tax and accounting law coverage.

Low-Cost Alternatives

If you balked at the prices mentioned for Westlaw and LexisNexis in Chapter 4, then these low-cost alternatives are right up your alley. They try to be all-purpose aggregators like the Big Two, counting on their relative cheapness to make them attractive: The most expensive plan might run $995—that's per year. Of course, all you will get is primary authority (e.g., cases, statutes, and maybe regulations). What you will lack are indexing, secondary sources, and the sophisticated search engines of the Big Two.

Fastcase is the most popular low-cost alternative. According to its website, Fastcase includes "primary law from all 50 states, as well as deep federal coverage going back to 1 U.S. 1, 1 F.2d 1, 1 F.Supp. 1, and 1 B.R. 1. The Fastcase collection includes cases, statutes, regulations, court rules, and constitutions. Fastcase also provides access to a newspaper archive, legal forms, and a one-stop PACER search of federal filings through our content partners."[7] It doesn't have all the secondary sources of Westlaw or Lexis, and the search engine is less sophisticated, but Fastcase does have some nice features:

- Keyword, natural language, and citation searches
- Google-like relevance ranking of results (can be customized in several other ways)
- The ability to jump right to most relevant paragraph of any document
- Integrated research history
- The ability to save documents for later

Let's go back to my search for copyright cases involving J. D. Salinger. Figure 6.3 shows the first three Fastcase (www.fast case.com) results. Note that the circuit court opinion, *Salinger v. Random House*, 811 F.2d 90, is not the first result; instead, it's the district court opinion, 650 F.Supp. 413 (S.D.N.Y. 1986). Westlaw and LexisNexis gave me the circuit opinion first. Clicking on the first result here gives me the full opinion. There are no headnotes or key numbers, of course, though other cases cited in the opinion are hyperlinked. I can print or email the case, and I can even run an authority check (i.e., *Shepard's* or KeyCite) for an additional charge. The homepage also lists legal forms (via www.uslegal

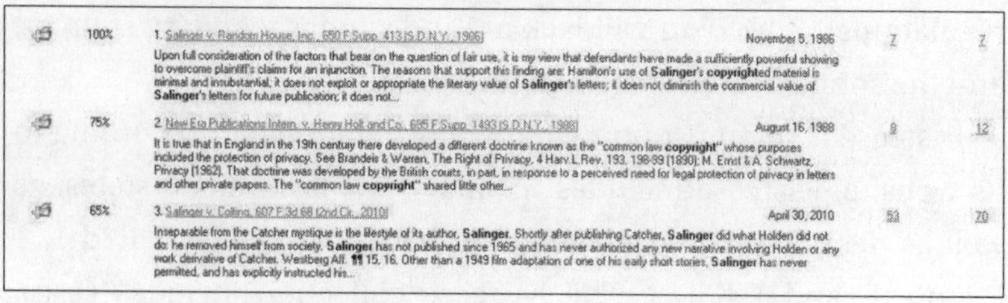

100% 1. Salinger v. Random House, Inc., 650 F.Supp. 413 (S.D.N.Y., 1986) November 5, 1986 7 7

Upon full consideration of the factors that bear on the question of fair use, it is my view that defendants have made a sufficiently powerful showing to overcome plaintiff's claims for an injunction. The reasons that support this finding are: Hamilton's use of **Salinger**'s **copyright**ed material is minimal and insubstantial; it does not exploit or appropriate the literary value of **Salinger**'s letters; it does not diminish the commercial value of **Salinger**'s letters for future publication; it does not...

75% 2. New Era Publications Intern. v. Henry Holt and Co., 695 F.Supp. 1493 (S.D.N.Y., 1988) August 16, 1988 8 12

It is true that in England in the 19th century there developed a different doctrine known as the "common law **copyright**" whose purposes included the protection of privacy. See Brandeis & Warren, The Right of Privacy, 4 Harv.L.Rev. 193, 198-99 (1890); M. Ernst & A. Schwartz, Privacy (1962). That doctrine was developed by the British courts, in part, in response to a perceived need for legal protection of privacy in letters and other private papers. The "common law **copyright**" shared little other...

65% 3. Salinger v. Colting, 607 F.3d 68 (2nd Cir., 2010) April 30, 2010 53 70

Inseparable from the Catcher mystique is the lifestyle of its author, **Salinger**. Shortly after publishing Catcher, **Salinger** did what Holden did not do: he removed himself from society. **Salinger** has not published since 1965 and has never authorized any new narrative involving Holden or any work derivative of Catcher. Westberg Aff. ¶¶ 15, 16. Other than a 1949 film adaptation of one of his early short stories, **Salinger** has never permitted, and has explicitly instructed his...

Figure 6.3 Top Fastcase results for J. D. Salinger copyright search

forms.com, a do-it-yourself website), federal filings, and newspapers as searchable databases.

Fastcase makes no effort to compete with Wexis on quality or service; price is its only draw. For some small firms, however, low price is the *sine qua non*. Lawyers lucky enough to belong to one of the company's 18 bar association partners[8] can pay *nothing* for the service. Most law firm librarians can ignore Fastcase—law firms large enough to employ a librarian will also subscribe to Westlaw or LexisNexis—but public librarians should be familiar with it. For public libraries that want to give patrons access to legal information, Fastcase or another one of the following low-cost alternatives, is increasingly the way to go:

- Versuslaw (www.versuslaw.com) costs less than $500 per year, covers federal and state case law (federal district opinions back to 1950) plus statutes, and has a complete content list on its website.
- Loislaw (www.loislaw.com) offers various plans that include all federal primary law, all federal law plus primary law for one state, or all federal and all state primary law, and some plans that include full-text treatises published by CCH or Aspen (CCH owns Aspen and Loislaw). It includes GlobalCite, a citator similar to Shepard's and KeyCite but much less developed.

Free Legal Websites

As with any subject, there are hundreds of thousands of websites, online research guides, and blogs devoted to law. Some are excellent, some execrable. Blogs and research guides are discussed in Chapter 9. Here, I offer some of the best general law-related sites.

FindLaw

Owned by West (and what isn't these days?), FindLaw (www.find law.com) has both a consumer and a professional portal (Figure 6.4). The professional site is rich in how-to articles on law firm marketing, billing and finance, technology, careers, and other concerns. It is also a database, though an incomplete one, of federal and state primary law. Case law seems to go back to the mid-1990s for most jurisdictions (except the U.S. Supreme Court, which starts in 1893), and FindLaw provides just the text of the opinions—no headnotes, key numbers, or other research aids. The *U.S. Code* is there, as are statutes for nine of the 50 states. For the remainder, FindLaw links to that state legislature's website, where the statutes can be found.

HG.org

Like FindLaw, HG.org (www.hg.org) has lots of news and practical advice for working attorneys (Figure 6.5). It is also a great marketplace for lawyer support services and professional organizations (FindLaw has this component, too). Two things distinguish HG.org, however. One is its research guides, which cover 260 areas of law, some so specialized (e.g., cell phone accidents, equine law, and prostitution law) that they aren't covered anywhere else. The other is its international coverage. The legal systems of more than 150 countries are covered, as well as the United Nations, NAFTA, the World Bank, and other organizations.

Figure 6.4   FindLaw homepage

Figure 6.5   HG.org homepage

WashLaw

WashLaw (www.washlaw.edu) is another gateway site, similar to FindLaw. Maintained by librarians at the Washburn University School of Law, WashLaw has better state coverage than other sites (Figure 6.6). If I click on California, for example, I see links to:

- Statutes and administrative regs

- All trial and appellate courts

- Fifty-eight administrative boards and 41 state commissions

- Fifty executive departments

- Twenty law libraries

- Civil and criminal jury instructions

- State and federal court forms

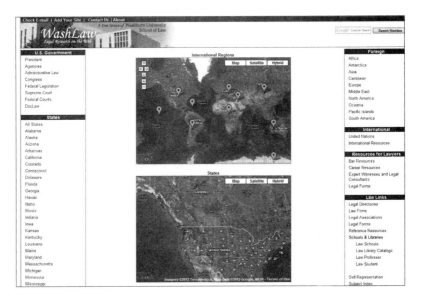

Figure 6.6   International Regions section of the WashLaw site

THOMAS

THOMAS (thomas.loc.gov) is a database of Congressional information maintained by the Library of Congress (Figure 6.7). It has the same type of legislative history information as ProQuest Congressional, but its coverage dates only from the mid-1990s. A few unique features include:

- A live Twitter feed
- Videos of House Floor Proceedings (www.houselive.gov)
- U.S. treaties back to 1967

The Library of Congress also maintains a full-text archive of Congressional documents from 1774 to 1875 titled A Century of Lawmaking for a New Nation (www.memory.loc.gov/ammem/ amlaw/lawhome.html). This archive is superior to ProQuest Congressional for this time period.

Zimmerman's Research Guide

Now owned by Lexis—and what isn't these days, other than the stuff owned by West?—Zimmerman's Research Guide (law.lexis nexis.com/infopro/zimmermans) was started by Andrew Zimmerman, a law librarian. The guide

> began several years ago when I [Zimmerman] was visiting a senior law librarian at her office. In the middle of our conversation she opened a drawer and pointed to a black ring binder stuffed with paper. This was her "black book." She said the binder held twenty-odd years of her accumulated wisdom. Then she closed the drawer, and I never saw the book again.
>
> That afternoon I started my own black book. Mostly I just took notes on anything I learned in the library. At first I kept my notes to myself, but soon I started printing out

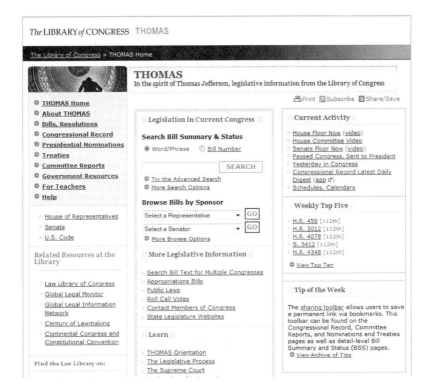

Figure 6.7   THOMAS homepage

copies for other librarians. I called the manuscript "A Reference Guide."[9]

Zimmerman published the guide online in 1999 and has maintained it ever since. Basically, it is an encyclopedia of legal terms, but from a law librarian perspective (Figure 6.8). For example, if you look up *attorney general opinions*, you don't get a definition of this term; rather, you get a list of places where attorney general opinions can be found. The guide is your cheat sheet when an attorney asks for something that to her is second-nature but to you is a mystery:

Figure 6.8   Zimmerman's Research Guide main page

Question: I need a copy of Bank of America's latest comfort letter.

Answer (after stealthily consulting Zimmerman's entry on comfort letters): Do you mean the latest letter from its auditors or one the SEC has issued to close an investigation? Both are private and not usually published anywhere, but I'll see what I can do.[10]

Public Library of Law

The Public Library of Law (PLOL; www.plol.org) is Fastcase's free law site. The clean, Google-like interface (Figure 6.9) will appeal to some researchers; otherwise, there isn't much different about

Figure 6.9   Public Library of Law homepage

PLOL. Only the case law tab seems to draw from the Fastcase database. The other tabs—statutes, regulations, court rules, constitutions, and legal forms—just link to other websites.

Law.Gov

"Law.Gov is an idea," states the organization's homepage (law.resource.org; Figure 6.10), "an idea that the primary legal materials of the United States should be readily available to all, and that governmental institutions should make these materials available in bulk as distributed, authenticated, well-formatted data." To that end, Carl Malamud, founder of the Internet

Multicasting Service and chief technology officer at the Center for American Progress, created Public.Resource.org in 2007 to house free databases of U.S. government documents, including case law. Malamud started with Volume 1 of West's *Federal Reporter* and has been working his way forward.[11] It is a nice idea, perhaps, but one that others are doing better. The *U.S. Code* and all state statutes are already online, and Congressional materials, recent and remote, are available through THOMAS and the Century of Lawmaking archive. Law.Gov offers no indexing, no searching, not even a table

Figure 6.10 Law.Gov homepage

of cases. As an antigovernment stunt, it isn't bad, but as a research database, it is useless (see Chapter 10 for more discussion).

Google Scholar

In 2009, Google began adding case law to its Google Scholar database (www.scholar.google.com). The database now includes:

- State appellate cases since 1950

- U.S. district, appellate, tax, and bankruptcy cases since 1923

- U.S. Supreme Court cases since 1791

In addition, Google Scholar includes "citations for cases cited by indexed opinions or journal articles which allows you to find influential cases (usually older or international) which are not yet online or publicly available" (see www.scholar.google.com/intl/en/scholar/about.html). The best feature, though, is Google's state-of-the-art search engine, which, as discussed in Chapter 5, Westlaw and LexisNexis have emulated in WestlawNext and Lexis Advance.

Google has changed the way research is done. How might it change legal research? Today's law school students grew up with Google. They know its blank backdrop, multicolored logo, and wide-mouthed search bar better than anything else. The old complicated interfaces of Westlaw and LexisNexis don't appeal to them. Plus, Westlaw and LexisNexis are so darn expensive, especially to those same students when they become new lawyers. So if there was ever a time when the Big Two were vulnerable, it is now.

Google, however, is not a serious threat. For starters, all it has are cases and journals. Few attorneys can make a practice without access to statutes, regulations, treatises, briefs, or other materials. In addition, Google only includes published cases. Unpublished ones can't always be cited, but they are often useful when preparing your own case. Plus, opposing counsel may refer to one, which you would need to get your hands on in a hurry.

Not only does Google have less content, but that content is also updated more slowly in comparison to Westlaw and LexisNexis. For example, Google lists the same coverage of state opinions (since 1950) and of U.S. district and circuit ones (since 1923) as it did when it first appeared in 2009. Finally, though the Google brand dominates the web in general, the world of electronic legal research has for the last three decades come down to two names: West and Lexis. I can't see *any* company ever unseating them.

But Google doesn't want to unseat West and Lexis. Google's competitors are other free sites, such as those mentioned earlier in this chapter. Many of them have a big head start, but I can see Google catching up. It has the expertise, the technology, and the money to do so, and its first effort in the market is not bad. Not bad at all.

Mobile Legal Research Apps

Every year, the American Bar Association's (ABA) Legal Technology Resource Center surveys attorneys about their use of information technology, both in the office and in the courtroom. In 2010, the survey found that 76 percent of respondents use smartphones, up from 64 percent in the 2009 survey. The BlackBerry was the most popular (66 percent), followed by the iPhone (20 percent) and Palm Pilot (9 percent).[12] More than a third of respondents (35 percent) reported regularly conducting research away from their offices.[13] In the 2011 survey, 27 percent of respondents said they had downloaded a law-specific app for their phones. The most popular app? Surprisingly, it was Fastcase (25 percent), which was downloaded by 11 percent and 9 percent respectively.[14]

Put these facts together, and it is clear that attorneys are using all types of handheld devices for legal research. Though in-depth research and document review are still best completed on wider-screened desktops or laptops, mobile devices are well suited for quick searches or citation retrievals. These searches can occur anywhere—home, street corner, coffee shop, even in court. When a dispute arises over the language of a case or statute, an attorney can bring up the document *right then* for a resolution.

Westlaw

West has offered a mobile version of Westlaw for nearly 10 years. Accessible through an app or customized mobile site at no extra charge, its features include:

- All primary and secondary sources
- KeyCite
- Searching by terms and connectors or by natural language
- Emailing of results to five people at once
- Printing to a stand-alone Westlaw printer

Westlaw is available for iPad (info.legalsolutions.thomson reuters.com/westlawnext/mobile-ipad/ipad-app/default.aspx) and Android devices (info.legalsolutions.thomsonreuters.com/ westlawnext/mobile-ipad/android-app/default.aspx), and its mobile site works on iOS, Android, BlackBerry, Windows Phone, and Amazon Kindle Fire.

LexisNexis

LexisNexis's mobile version, Lexis Advance, allows:

- Instant search (run a search without having to select a specific source; filter answers by jurisdiction, date, topic, keyword, or court)
- Access to *Shepard's*

- Work folders (save searches, results, and Shepard's reports)

- Bookmarking and emailing of documents

Other apps available from LexisNexis include:

- Legal News and Legal News Briefs

- Courtlink (for reviewing new court dockets and tracking docket activity)

- eBooks (Matthew Bender treatises for downloading to phone or ereader)

- Accurint Public records searches

- Get Cases & Shepardize

- Law School Q&A series (multiple-choice and essay questions, plus answers)

- Lead Alert (real-time notifications of new client leads)

- Tax Law Community (tax news, analysis, and commentary, including blogs and podcasts)

- Nexis News Search

- Lawyers.com

Lexis Advance is available for the iPhone and iPad, and its mobile site (www.lexisnexis.com/en-us/products/mobile.page) works on iOS, Android, BlackBerry, Windows Phone, and Amazon Kindle Fire.

Fastcase

Download the free iPhone app from www.fastcase.com/ipad or the Android app from www.fastcase.com/android. Until recently, Fastcase apps were *not* synced with a Fastcase online account. A user's search history and saved documents on the app would not appear when that user logged in to Fastcase online, and vice-versa. Now the two can be synced (www.fastcase.com/mobile-sync).

Another recent Fastcase innovation is advance sheets for state and federal cases. These include published and unpublished opinions, distinguishing Fastcase from West reporters. The advance sheets are available for iPad, Kindle, Nook, and Android devices (www.fastcase.com/ebooks).

HeinOnline

The William S. Hein Company has offered mobile access to its HeinOnline database since 2008. Hein's mobile access allows you to retrieve documents by citation, browse law reviews and journals, search the full text of documents, and view PDF copies. At this time, it is available for iPad and iPhone only, and you must have a HeinOnline subscription to use the app (home.heinon line.org/heinonline-app).

Other Mobile Apps

The UCLA School of Law Library has an excellent guide (libguides.law.ucla.edu/mobilelegalapps) to mobile applications designed for legal research, law school and bar exam study, and productivity. Here are some of the legal research apps:

- ABA Journal, a free app for iPhone, iPod Touch, and iPad: Provides breaking legal news and articles featured in the *ABA Journal.* May be downloaded from the iTunes App Store (www.tinyurl.com/yl2oulp).

- American Lawyer, a free app for iPhone and iPad: Provides instant access to recent issues of *American Lawyer* every month. May be downloaded from the iTunes App Store.

- Black's Law Dictionary: Available for the iPhone and iPad and can be bought from the iTunes App Store. A version for Android devices can be purchased at www.blackslaw dictionary.com/Home/Android.aspx.

- Courtroom Objections: Based on the *Federal Rules of Evidence* and *Texas Rules of Evidence*, offers explanations of and suggested language for common objections to admissibility and form. By scrolling past the explanation, you can view the relevant rule of evidence. Purchase for the iPad, iPhone, and iPod Touch devices from the iTunes App Store.

- Droidlaw: Search, bookmark, copy, share, and annotate the text of the *Federal Rules of Civil Procedure, Evidence, Appellate Procedure, Criminal Procedure,* and *Bankruptcy Procedure* using an Android device. The app is free and available at www.droidlaw.com. Various add-ons such as the *U.S. Code, Code of Federal Regulations (CFR)*, and Supreme Court opinions are available for purchase.

- LawStack: Similar to Droidlaw, except the *U.S. Code* and *CFR* are free add-ons.

- Legal News Reader: An RSS feed aggregator that retrieves important news stories from a number of legal news sites. Users can comment on articles and read others' comments. Purchase from the iTunes App Store.

- Mobile Transcript: With this app, read deposition transcripts formatted for their devices. Court reporters upload transcripts to the Mobile Transcript website (www.mobiletranscript.com/transcript), which downloads them to attorneys' mobile devices. Also allows users to highlight and flag text.

- OpenRegs: Lets you track significant regulations published in the *Federal Register*, locate recently issued notices of final and proposed rule-making, and browse regulations by agency or comment period. App is free from the iTunes App Store.

- TyMetrixRateDriver: Allows users to search law firm billing rates in major U.S. markets. A free 60-day trial is available. May be downloaded from the iTunes App Store, www.android.com for Android devices, and www.us.blackberry.com/apps-software/appworld for BlackBerry devices.

Endnotes

1. Greg Lambert, "Information Wants to be Free—But, We'll Still Pay for 'Authority,'" 3 Geeks and a Law Blog (blog), August 13, 2009, accessed November 26, 2012, www.geeklawblog.com/2009/08/information-wants-to-be-free-but-well.html.
2. Ibid.
3. "ProQuest Acquires Acclaimed Congressional Information Service and University Publications of America from LexisNexis," November 30, 2010, accessed November 26, 2012, www.proquest.com/en-US/aboutus/pressroom/10/20101130.shtml.
4. For a good discussion of the principles of statutory interpretation, including the use of legislative history, see Yule Kim, "Statutory Interpretation: General Principles and Recent Trends," Open CRS, August 31, 2008, accessed November 26, 2012, www.opencrs.com/document/97-589.
5. "Milestones 1920s–1930s," Bloomberg BNA, accessed November 26, 2012, www.bna.com/bna-milestones-1920s1930s-a8589934750.
6. "Bloomberg Completes Acquisition of BNA," Bloomberg BNA, September 30, 2011, accessed November 26, 2012, www.bna.com/bloomberg-completes-acquisition-pr12884903683.
7. "What Is Fastcase?" Fastcase.com, accessed November 26, 2012, www.fastcase.com/whatisfastcase.
8. For a list of these, see www.fastcase.com/barmembers.
9. Andrew Zimmerman, "About Zimmerman's Research Guide," Zimmerman's Research Guide, accessed November 26, 2012, law.lexisnexis.com/infopro/zimmermans/about.aspx.
10. See Andrew Zimmerman, "Comfort Letters," Zimmerman's Research Guide, accessed November 26, 2012, law.lexisnexis.com/infopro/zimmermans/disp.aspx?z=1307.

11.   Is this a copyright violation? See https://public.resource.org/scribd/ 3319367.pdf for West's informative but condescending reply to a letter from Malamud on this topic.

12.   "ABA Legal Technology Survey Results Released," abanow.org, September 28, 2010, accessed November 26, 2012, www.abanow. org/2010/09/aba-legal-technology-survey-results-released.

13.   Ibid.

14.   Catherine Sanders Reach, "ABA Legal Technology Survey Adds New Devices, Technologies," *Law Technology News*, July 12, 2011, accessed November 26, 2012, www.law.com/jsp/lawtechnology news/PubArticleLTN.jsp?id=1202499792646.

Where's Waldo?: Public Information Searches for Law Librarians

Remember the movie *The Net*? Sandra Bullock plays the role of Angela Bennet, a software analyst who stumbles upon a floppy disk belonging to the Praetorians, a gang of cyberterrorists. One of the terrorists, Jack Devlin, played with creepy élan by Jeremy Northam, tries to romance the disk out of Angela. When that doesn't work, he erases her. Cancels her credit cards. Crashes her best friend's plane. Sells her house. Gives her a new name and passport plus a criminal record, which leads to her arrest. Sitting in jail, she babbles to her court-appointed attorney, "Our whole world is sitting there on a computer … your DMV records, your Social Security [number], your credit cards, your medical history. It's all right there; everyone is stored in there. It's like this little electronic shadow on each and every one of us just begging for somebody to screw with."

Here's the weird thing about *The Net*: It was science fiction. The movie was made in 1995, when cybercrime was as far-fetched as Klingons and Romulans. Watching it now, we laugh at the primitive websites that Angela visits and the bottle-sized cell phone that Devlin holds to his ear. But we don't laugh at the "little electronic shadow." Identity theft is the new shoplifting. The Federal Trade Commission estimates that as many as 9 million Americans have their identity stolen every year.[1]

As a law librarian, I have often used the internet to locate public information, though not for nefarious reasons. There are plenty of bona fide reasons to pursue that electronic shadow. Courts need to find people to serve subpoenas. Managers have to do background checks on job applicants. Banks want credit reports before lending money. I have also been asked to find information on specific companies or their executives, usually to assist my law firm's marketing or business development efforts (see Chapter 8).

Public Information

Types of public information include:

- Birth and death certificates
- Marriage licenses
- Asset sales (e.g., cars, boats, airplanes, stocks)
- Internet directories
- Voter registrations
- Political contributions
- Civil and criminal filings
- Liens, judgments, and UCC filings[2]
- Real estate sales
- Property records
- Professional licenses (e.g., lawyer, doctor, architect, plumber, mortician, cosmetologist)
- Corporation filings
- Motor vehicle records
- Foundation and charity donor records
- Social media sites (e.g., Facebook, LinkedIn)

The following books and websites are great tools to begin a search for public information.

Helpful books include:

- Levitt, Carole A. and Mark E. Rosch. *Find Info Like a Pro, Volume 1: Mining the Internet's Publicly Available Resources for Investigative Research.* Chicago: American Bar Association, 2010.

- Levitt, Carole A. and Mark E. Rosch. *Find Info Like a Pro, Volume 2: Mining the Internet's Public Records for Investigative Research.* Chicago: American Bar Association, 2012.

- Sankey, Michael and Peter Weber. *The Sourcebook to Public Record Information: The Comprehensive Guide to County, State, & Federal Public Records Sources,* 10th ed. Tempe, AZ: BRB Publications, 2009.

Useful websites are:

- BRB Publications (www.brbpub.com): Several free sources plus books and electronic products pointing the way to over 26,000 government agencies and 3,500 public records vendors

- Business Intelligence Online Resources (www.llrx.com/ features/busintellguide.htm): Dozens of sites useful for business and company research

- Finding People Online (www.libraryspot.com/features/ peoplefeature.htm): Guide to tracking down those who have tried to disappear

- Gumshoe Librarian (www.llrx.com/features/gum shoe.htm): Bibliography of websites useful for locating people

- How to Find People on the Web (websearch.about.com/od/peoplesearch/tp/peoplesearch.htm): Another guide to finding people

- SearchSystems.net (www.searchsystems.net): Over 38,000 databases containing business information, corporate filings, property records, deeds, mortgages, criminal and civil court filings, records on inmates and offenders, births, deaths, and marriages, unclaimed property records, professional licenses, and more (subscriptions cost less than $50 per year, making this one of the least expensive in the industry)

- State and Local Government on the Net (www.statelocal gov.net): Over 8,000 official state, county, or city government websites

- Virtual Chase (www.virtualchase.com): Articles on public records, locating corporate information, and finding people

- Virtual Gumshoe (www.virtualgumshoe.com): Maintained by a pair of private investigators, over 4,000 public information databases (most of the site is free, although there are services—e.g., a 24-hour criminal record check—that require payment)

Company Information

The old saw of law librarianship is that the litigators keep the library in business. Litigation, civil or criminal, is when attorneys are researching cases and statutes, studying concepts, and developing theories. Transactional attorneys, those handling mergers, acquisitions, restructurings, and other business deals, rarely darken the door of the library—except when they need information on a particular company.

The obvious place to start such research is a company's website, where you can learn a lot. I was once asked to discern the relationship between two companies: Nan Ya Technology and Formosa Plastics Group. On the website of Formosa Plastics Group, I found a diagram of its corporate structure. The diagram named Nan Ya Technology Corp. and Nan Ya Plastics Corp. as "local companies" with a hard-line direct report to the president of Formosa Plastics. This suggested that both Nan Ya companies were owned by Formosa Plastics.

Other requests aren't so straightforward. For a company overview, you need a strategy. I recommend the following five steps:

1. Look for information on the company executives.

2. Locate the company's financial information (e.g., SEC filings, current and historical stock prices, analyst reports).[3]

3. Check news databases for mentions of the company.

4. Examine the company's interest or involvement in legislative or regulatory actions.

5. Find out the public opinion of the company.

There are several commercial databases useful for company (and personal) research and background investigations:

- Accurint (www.accurint.com): Owned by Lexis; offers access to over 34 billion public records

- CLEAR (www.clear.thomsonreuters.com): Originally known as ChoicePoint (a term you might still hear); acquired in 2008 by Thomson West; maintains records on businesses and individuals; benefits from the top-of-the-line West search engine technology

- Dun & Bradstreet (www.dnb.com): In business since 1841, the oldest company of this type; maintains records on over 200 million companies worldwide

- Hoover's (www.hoovers.com): A subsidiary of Dun & Bradstreet; maintains records on over 60 million companies (also has records on individuals); has less-detailed records free of charge on its website

In a midsize firm or public library, however, you will probably not have access to these. The following are some good free websites.[4] For finding company executives:

- CPA Directory (www.cpadirectory.com): Contains the names and addresses of 450,000 certified public accountants in the U.S.; from the homepage, searchable by name and state (city is optional)

- Executive Paywatch (www.aflcio.org/corporate-watch/ CEO-Pay-and-the-99/CEO-Pay-Data-Sources): An executive compensation database; searchable by company name or ticker symbol, or look at the list of 100 highest-paid executives

- Ziggs (www.ziggs.com): More than 1 million executive profiles from 15,000 companies and 40 industries; searchable by last or first name, city/state, company, or keyword

For finding financial filings:

- 10K Wizard (www.10kwizard.com): SEC filings made since 1994; a useful feature includes searching for model language that appears in all types of filings[5]

- Big Charts (www.bigcharts.com): Historical single-day stock quotes back to 1988; also offers comparative NYSE, NASDAQ, and AMEX reports; advanced tools available to paid subscribers

- EDGAR (www.sec.gov/edgar.shtml): Official database of SEC filings; includes only searchable data found in the header of the document

- Investing in Bonds (www.investinginbonds.com): Historical trading data for municipal bonds, as well as daily corporate bond transactions and composite treasury reports

- Yahoo! Finance (finance.yahoo.com): One-stop shop for company and market information; links to historical stock prices (some back to 1960s), analyst reports, financials, and news

For finding news stories:

- American City Business Journals (www.bizjournals.com): News by industry, region, or keyword; email news alerts available

- Bloomberg.com (www.bloomberg.com): Mix of free and fee-based news stories on markets, economies, and companies around the world; special feature provides current stock information, found by entering a ticker symbol

- Corporate Crime Reporter (www.corporatecrime reporter.com): Subscription newsletter reporting on lawsuits, agency actions, and other events; lists the top 100 corporations charged with crimes, hot documents (e.g., Martha Stewart's 2004 indictment for lying to federal investigators), interviews with white-collar crime defense lawyers, and more

- I Want Media (www.iwantmedia.com): Directory of news sources and organizations; also links to about a dozen good research sites

- Television News Archive (www.tvnews.vanderbilt.edu): Abstracts of evening news stories and special reports back to 1968

- U.S. Newspaper List (www.usnpl.com): Websites of newspapers, radio stations, and TV stations in all 50 states; also lists sites for stock quotes, maps, weather, and more

For finding information on legal or regulatory activity:

- Analysis and Information Online (ai.volpe.dot.gov/mcspa.asp): Single point of entry to transportation-related databases, where you can find extensive statistics (e.g., 14 percent of those killed in large truck crashes in 1999 were the truck's occupants)

- Congressional Record (thomas.loc.gov): Transcripts of debates on the floor of Congress (Congressmen often read a company's written remarks into the record); also available through ProQuest Congressional database (see Chapter 6)

- Corporate Registration, The National Association of Secretaries of State (www.nass.org/busreg/corpreg.html): State sites with information about registering for-profit and nonprofit corporations

- FreeERISA.com (www.freeerisa.com): Free reference databases of companies' Form 5500 filings, Form 5310 filings, pension funds, and SEC filings; also has a library of National Labor Relations Board decisions, collective bargaining agreements, and more

- MedWATCH (www.fda.gov/safety/MedWatch/default.htm): Clinical information about safety issues involving drugs, biologics, radiation-emitting devices, and nutritional products; browsable by safety alerts or company name

- NLRB Decisions (nlrb.gov/cases-decisions): National Labor Relations Board decisions from 1996 to present

- SEC Enforcement Division (www.sec.gov/divisions/enforce.shtml): Litigation releases, administrative proceedings, notices about trading suspensions, investor alerts, and more

- WebBRD (lopucki.law.ucla.edu): Database of public company bankruptcies beginning in 1980

For finding information on public opinion:

- BBB Reviews (www.bbb.org/us/Find-Business-Reviews): Database of business and clarity reviews by the Better Business Bureau

- CorpWatch (www.corpwatch.org): Reports on corporate activities worldwide; tips and strategies for finding information about companies, public or private

- Google Groups (groups.google.com): Newsgroup messages since 1981; searching for company or executive names to see what people have been saying

- ResellerRatings.com (www.resellerratings.com): Consumer opinions about online vendors for computer hardware or software; the vendors are rated accordingly

- Yahoo! Consumer Opinion (www.snipurl.com/d8ys): Websites devoted to public opinion

Individual Persons

Searching for information on an individual person may seem overwhelming, so plan your search before you sit down at the computer. Here are some tips to keep in mind:

- Know what you need. Most searches are simple: an address, phone number, or date of birth. You can find this free on the internet.

- Consider a low-tech approach. Call friends, relatives, clubs, churches, or former employers of the person you're looking for. If you have an old address, send an envelope marked "Address Correction Requested/Do Not Forward." The post office will label the envelope with the current address and return it to you.

- Understand that some information, such as credit histories, Social Security numbers, and motor vehicle records, is never free.

- Don't trust pay databases implicitly. All databases have errors, so verify (if you can) what you find in them. In 2005, for example, the public records vendor ChoicePoint[6] made headlines for having legions of errors in its database. One woman's profile showed cars she had never owned and employers for which she had never worked. Another man read his profile and learned that he died in 1976.

To Strive, to Seek, to Find

Have you ever Googled yourself? I do it every few months. Usually, I find articles I've written or the website of the university where I teach. However, I've also found the car salesman in Mt. Gilead, Ohio, who shares my name. Once, I found my grandmother's newspaper obituary, which I had not yet seen.

When you're searching for a person, it's tempting to start with Google, but I don't recommend this. Besides Arnold Schwarzenegger, few people have a name so uncommon that Google will suss them out. Better to start with White Pages (www.whitepages.com) or a similar site, all of which work by searching telephone directory listings.

The drawback to this is obvious: People who skip bail, break their lease, or fail to pay loans probably also don't publish their addresses and phone numbers. However, when you need to find regular people, White Pages can give you a lead.

Suppose I want to find my ex-girlfriend, Jamie Hunter, so I can return her stuff that I recently found in my closet. When I last saw Jamie, her company was about to transfer her to Baton Rouge, Louisiana. I go to AnyWho (www.anywho.com), type her name, choose LA from the drop-down box, and—bingo! Only one Jamie Hunter comes up.

But what if my Jamie has moved? What if she has an unlisted phone number? What if she is married and has a different last name? What if she married, changed her last name, divorced, and changed her name *back*? How do I know whether this Jamie Hunter is the one I want?

To the right of the screen, I see a list of reports I can buy (see Figure 7.1).

Find more information from Intelius

More Information for Jamie P Hunter
» Email and Other Phone Lookup
» Get Detailed Background Information
» Get Public Records
» View Property & Area Information
» View Social Network Profile

More Information for Jamie Hunter
» Email and Other Phone Lookup
» Get Detailed Background Information
» Get Public Records
» View Property & Area Information
» View Social Network Profile

Figure 7.1   Reports available to buy after a person search

The reports range from $1.95 for an email address to $49.95 for a complete background check. Would I consider buying one of these reports? If I wanted to find her badly enough, sure. If I choose to buy a report, however, I need to buy several from different vendors. Why? Remember the ChoicePoint problem: Vendor databases have errors. Looking at one report, I don't know what is accurate, but if I look at several and see the same information in each one, that information is likely correct.

Similarly, I always keep a log of my searches, noting every person I talk to and every website I visit. Then I compare each new search result to what I've written in my log and look for consistencies as well as contradictions. There are thousands of websites I could have started with, many of which are mentioned in the tools at the beginning of this chapter. The key to finding people, however, is *not* which site you use; it is how you analyze the findings.

Another key: Be creative. I knew a woman who was trying to locate her ex-husband because he was behind on child support payments. She checked his voter registration and that of the woman he had left her for—all states make voter databases available online—and she noticed that both had changed to the same voting district. This implied the two had moved in together. Thinking they might be engaged, my friend checked with department stores in that area and located their bridal registry, which gave her their address and phone number.

Finding Waldo

Suppose you are the librarian for a firm defending a physician accused of medical malpractice. In treating a patient who had a temporary pacemaker, the physician failed to provide anticoagulant therapy, and the patient died from a stroke. You find a case where the same thing happened, and the case mentions a Dr. Albert Waldo who served as an expert witness. Your firm wants Dr.

Waldo for its witness, but first you need to locate him, check his credentials, and find out what he's done the last few years.

Again, you could pay for this at many site, such as Healthgrades (www.physicianreports.com), MDNationwide (www.mdnation wide.org), and DocInfo (www.docinfo.org). If you are unable or unwilling to pay, however, you can find a lot of information free online by conducting a "Where's Waldo?" search.

Despite my earlier importuning, you should start this search with Google. Why? Because you want to know Dr. Waldo professionally, not personally, and if he has a website, your search is half over. You run the search and come up with Dr. Waldo's address and phone number at the UH Case Medical Center (see Figure 7.2).

This contact information, however, isn't enough. Before calling the good doctor, your firm will want to check his reputation and his expertise. After all, the reason some doctors turn to the expert witness gig is because their credentials have been stripped. Better visit the State of Ohio Medical Board at www.med.ohio.gov and run a search. You find Dr. Waldo's name, address, and education, followed by the most important info: No formal action on his record. This means he has been found guilty of no professional malpractice. In other words, he isn't a quack (see Figure 7.3).

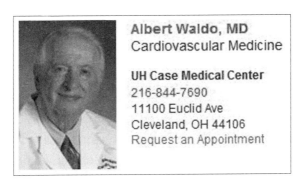

Figure 7.2   Listing for Dr. Albert Waldo

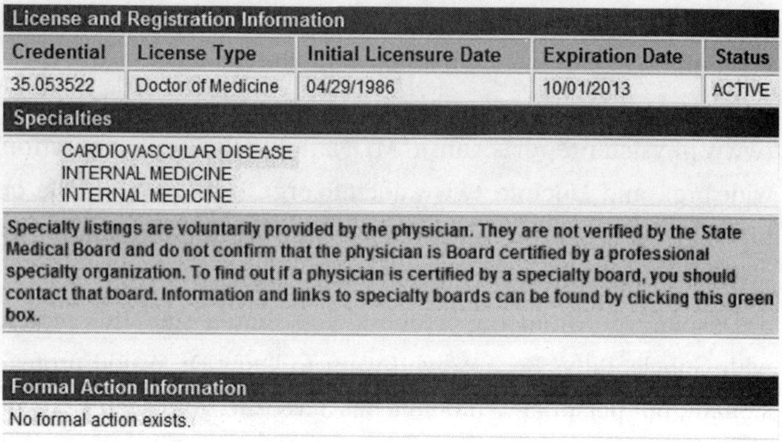

License and Registration Information				
Credential	**License Type**	**Initial Licensure Date**	**Expiration Date**	**Status**
35.053522	Doctor of Medicine	04/29/1986	10/01/2013	ACTIVE

Specialties

CARDIOVASCULAR DISEASE
INTERNAL MEDICINE
INTERNAL MEDICINE

Specialty listings are voluntarily provided by the physician. They are not verified by the State Medical Board and do not confirm that the physician is Board certified by a professional specialty organization. To find out if a physician is certified by a specialty board, you should contact that board. Information and links to specialty boards can be found by clicking this green box.

Formal Action Information

No formal action exists.

Figure 7.3   Dr. Waldo's license information

There is one more piece of information your attorneys will want: articles written by Dr. Waldo. I mean the dry-as-dust ones published in the medical journals no one reads. For that, go to www.pubmed.gov. Search for Dr. Waldo as the *first* author. Most medical articles are co-written, with the first author on the list having done the bulk of the research, making him or her the most knowledgeable about the study results. Figure 7.4 shows one of Dr. Waldo's articles as listed on PubMed. The article is not available in full text, so you will need to get this one via interlibrary loan.

Laws Governing Personal Information

Trying to find an old girlfriend or getting the lowdown on a physician seem like harmless, maybe even necessary, exercises of power, and they are, if you search only public sources of information such as newspapers, phone directories, or court filings. Commercial databases like those mentioned earlier, however, are off-limits unless you are a licensed professional or you have a legal interest in the search.

Cardiol Clin. 2009 Feb;27(1):125-35, ix.
Anticoagulation: stroke prevention in patients with atrial fibrillation.

Waldo AL.

Department of Medicine, Case Western Reserve University/University Hospitals of Cleveland Case Medical Center, 11100 Euclid Avenue, MS LKS 5038, Cleveland, OH 44106-5038, USA. albert.waldo@case.edu

Abstract
It is well recognized that during atrial fibrillation (AF), clots may form in the left atrium, which may embolize and cause ischemic stroke or systemic embolism. The presence of AF confers a fivefold increased risk for stroke. AF is the most common and important cause of stroke. This article considers the risks for and anticoagulation prophylaxis against embolic stroke in patients who have AF.

PMID: 19111789 [PubMed - indexed for MEDLINE]

Figure 7.4   PubMed entry for one of Dr. Waldo's articles

The following statutes regulate who may research a person's financial information and what that researcher may do with the results:

- Fair Credit Reporting Act, 15 U.S.C. § 1681 et seq.

- Fair Debt Collection Practices Act, 15 U.S.C. §§ 1692-1692p

- Gramm-Leach-Bliley Act, 15 U.S.C. §§ 6801-6809

You could also use a private investigator. PIs are regulated by most states. In North Carolina, for example, N.C.G.S. Chapter 74C is the Private Protective Services Act. The regulations implementing this Act can be found in 12 N.C.A.C. 7D. *PI Magazine* links to the private investigator laws for all 50 states.[7]

Courthouse Filings

Attorneys frequently ask for copies of filings—motions, complaints, answers, appellate briefs, and more—in actual court cases. One reason is these documents will list a person's name, address, occupation, place of employment, financial holdings, marital status, bankruptcies, and other useful information. With cases involving companies, you can find out about the officers and directors, the company's financial holdings, and more.

Another reason to obtain copies of filings is to use them as models for the attorney's own documents. West and Lexis publish books of forms for this purpose (see Chapter 2), but in my experience, attorneys always prefer a live document. Why? It has specific language and arguments they can adopt. Is this plagiarism? No. Court filings are public records, unprotected by copyright.

Westlaw and LexisNexis include many court filings, federal and state, in full text. These databases are among the most expensive, however, so small firms and public libraries tend not to have them. A cheaper source for U.S. appellate, district, and bankruptcy filings is Public Access to Court Electronic Records (PACER; www.pacer.gov), a service of the U.S. courts, which has over 500 million documents. Any member of the public can access PACER at a cost of 10 cents per page. Bills are sent quarterly, and if your access charges don't amount to $15.00 that quarter, then you pay nothing.

The states, as you might expect, have differing levels of access to civil and criminal filings. The National Center for State Courts has an excellent guide on this topic.[8] Older records are not available electronically, and no courthouse staff will find, copy, and send you documents. For these records, you will need to hire a runner, someone who will go to the courthouse and copy the documents for you. West has such a service (www.courtexpress.westlaw.com), as does Lexis (www.lexisnexis.com/courtlink). Both operate nationwide. Other, smaller companies limit themselves to one state (e.g., www.courthouserunners.com in South Florida) or one type of record (e.g., www.courthousedirect.com, specializing in property and bankruptcy records).

Appellate Briefs

Attorneys writing an appellate brief frequently want to study other briefs on the same topic. U.S. Supreme Court briefs are the easiest to find. Westlaw and LexisNexis have many, and some are available free online. Other federal briefs can be retrieved using PACER.

For state-level appellate briefs, start with state court websites, all of which are listed by the National Center for State Courts.[9] Another great source is the article "Free and Fee Based Appellate Court Briefs Online" by Michael Whiteman on LLRX (www.llrx. com/features/briefsonline.htm), listing free and commercial sources, as well as merits and amicus[10] briefs by various government agencies and nonprofit associations.

Endnotes

1. "Identity Theft," Crime Museum, accessed February 24, 2013, www. crimemuseum.org/Identity_Theft.html.
2. UCC stands for Uniform Commercial Code, a set of suggested laws relating to commercial transactions. The code was developed by the National Conference of Commissioners on Uniform State Laws, an independent group. Most states have adopted the code, though none are required to do so.
3. This is much easier for public companies (i.e., those traded on a stock exchange). Private companies are more elusive.
4. Website descriptions are adapted from resources available at www.virtualchase.justia.com.
5. Attorneys will often ask you for actual filings, contracts, or other documents to help them draft their own.
6. Now owned by Lexis. See https://personalreports.lexisnexis.com.
7. See the state license requirements at www.pimagazine.com/private_ investigator_license_requirements.html.
8. Links to state court filings databases, free and commercial, are available at www.ncsc.org/Topics/Access-and-Fairness/Privacy-Public-Access-to-Court-Records/State-Links.aspx.
9. All state court websites are available at www.ncsc.org/Information-and-Resources/Browse-by-State/State-Court-Websites.aspx.
10. *Amicus* means "friend of the court." Amicus briefs are filed not by the participants in a case but by interested trade groups or nonprofit associations who want the court to consider their interests. Usually, the court does not.

Chapter 8

The Anxiety of the Men (and Women) Inside the Board Rooms

In Chapter 1, you met Gabriel, the managing partner and well-known grump of a big law firm where I worked as a librarian. Gabriel was looking for some long-discontinued reporters that I had tossed, a breach I blamed on my predecessor. In Chapter 3, I sent Gabriel an ill-advised email, then compounded the problem by sending (gasp!) a second one. After the emails, I tried to keep a low profile. I didn't talk to Gabriel unless I had to, and when I passed him in the hallway, I averted my eyes. He came to my office every now and then with a request, and thank God I was able to meet them. Once, he asked me to locate a particular book for him. I found the book, walked it to his office … and left it with his secretary. Hey, I didn't need to have a brick wall fall on my head twice.

Things continued to work this way for 3 years until I left that firm. I got a going-away party on my last day in the biggest, plushest conference room. Attorneys and support staff stopped by to wish me well, grab some cookies and a can of soda, and drift back to their desks. Presently, Gabriel walked in with another partner. I assumed the partner was the one who wanted to see me off and that Gabriel just happened to be with him. Instead, Gabriel walked right up, looked me full in the face, shook my hand like an old friend, and said, "Man, I just can't believe you're leaving." (He sounded—what? Disappointed? Contrite? Guilty? Don't worry, Gabriel. I didn't leave because of you.)

Some law firms have a single librarian. My former firm had six of us spread across nine offices, with a seventh serving as the director of library services. She in turn reported to the chief operating officer, a nonlawyer business manager. Each office also had its own administrator (in my office, it was Preston). Administrators handle the business functions of a law office, but the ultimate authority rests with the firm-wide management committee, a group of partners elected to lead the firm. Similarly, in public libraries, the decision makers are boards of trustees. Both groups are charged with overseeing entities about which they know very little. Thus, an important skill for any law librarian is overcoming the anxiety of the men (and women) inside the board rooms.

Law Firm Administrators

Though Gabriel and I were never close, he no doubt saw my value to the firm he managed. "Savvy legal administrators," writes Katherine Rosin, "know that law librarians can provide a plethora of vital information, including data, statistics, articles, reports, surveys, government documents, links to websites and more."[1] A librarian's worth goes beyond data retrieval, however. We can "maximize [our] firms' knowledge bases and informational capabilities, thereby bolstering the firms' competitive edges, promoting the firms' businesses and boosting their profits."[2]

The profit mindset is key here. In library school, you mostly studied public libraries, academic libraries, and school media centers—in other words, not-for-profit outfits. These libraries' missions are centered on social good. The New York Public Library, for example, has as its mission "to inspire lifelong learning, advance knowledge, and strengthen our communities."[3] The mission of the University of San Francisco's Dorraine Zief Law Library is equally grandiose: "to pursue excellence in education, build a supportive, open learning community, and contribute to social justice as we strive to educate minds and hearts to change the world."[4]

Most law firm libraries have less august missions. A law firm is a business, and businesses exist to make money. Thus, a law firm library's *real* mission is to maximize shareholder profits (i.e., help the firm make money). Making money is a firm administrator's charge and the lens through which she views everything that happens in the firm. Therefore, the typical measures of library success—patron counts, number of check-outs, number of reference questions—will not impress firm management. Law firms are reducing, and sometimes closing, libraries left and right to cope with an uncertain economy. To avoid this fate, you must help the firm make money. Here are some ways to do it.

Bill Your Time

For most of us, it is a cliché to say that time is money. For law firm employees, however, time really is money in the form of billing rates. Fresh-from-law-school associates usually bill around $300 an hour. Senior partners? As high as $1,000 an hour. At the law firm where I worked, my time was worth $65 an hour. This was less than even the paralegals, which may sound as if I was undervalued. Yet the figure worked to my advantage: It helped me get work. Clients love attorneys who can save them money, and my low rate became a selling point. I was even able to increase my billable hours by 53 percent in my second year thanks to my client-friendly cost.

If you work for a firm that does not bill librarians' time, you need to change that. Now. There is no better way to showcase your value to the firm. Canceling the *Atlantic Reporter* gets you an atta-boy on your performance review. Putting 53 percent more money in the firm's coffers? Rock star status.

Be Conscious of Cost

In 2011, Greg Castanias, a partner at Jones Day, one of the world's largest law firms, spoke at a meeting of the American Association of Law Libraries about his perspective on law library value. "What you want to know and understand," he told the librarians, "is this: What makes [firm management] tick? What are the pressures they are facing in their job of managing the law firm? Are they perceiving you and the libraries as doing the things that need to be done to run a law firm at the highest level?" He then spelled out some of those things:

> Ask yourself the hard questions: Is my physical library space the right size? (Remember, real estate costs real money.) Is our physical collection the right size? Is our staff the right size? Are we really adding value, or are we a drain on the bottom line? (Perhaps just as importantly, are we perceived as adding core value, or are you perceived as a drain on the bottom line?)
>
> You can earn a heck of a lot of gold stars by going to management and saying things like "We don't need all of this space; would you like some of it back?" You can also mark yourself as the sort of person management likes (because you help them sleep better at night) by doing things like teaching lawyers how to use the free legal resources that are out there, like Google Scholar. Don't assume that everyone—or anyone—knows about these things. When I wrote an article for our firmwide library newsletter that talked about how I've come to use Google Scholar for most of my partner-level research needs (which these days is mostly pulling a case here or a case there), I got an astounding number of emails from everyone from new associates to senior partners thanking me for helping them practice law with more sensitivity to client cost controls. What I wrote, by the way, was that I can now use Google Scholar for about 95 percent of what I used to use

Westlaw or Lexis[Nexis] for, and about 80 percent of what I used those services for when I was an associate.[5]

Cost consciousness goes beyond canceling subscriptions and harassing publishers for discounts. It is a worldview that informs every decision the firm makes. Show the firm leaders that you share this worldview.

Recover Costs

Library books and periodicals are a fixed cost—their price is not based on usage. You buy books, and whether they sit unused for years or are thumbed through every day, you pay the same amount. Most databases don't work that way. Their prices are based on estimated usage, and as I explain in Chapter 5, that price can be increased on the basis of actual usage.

To defray database cost, most firms pass along some of it to their clients. Westlaw and LexisNexis have built-in features to enable this, and most attorneys are familiar with them. They are probably not familiar with cost recovery software such as Onelog (www.onelog.com) or LookUp Precision (www.lookup-precision.com). These programs sit on top of any of the firm's databases and prompt a user to enter a client billing number before accessing the database. The program then tracks the user's time on that database. It even works with free websites.

The advantage to the firm of cost recovery software is clear: When it is time to renew the database, you can renegotiate with the vendor based on actual usage data. You can also show that partner who claims, "But I use that database all the time" that, in fact, she has not used it all year, giving you leverage in cancellation discussions. What is the advantage of such software to *you*? It is a way to show the firm's managers that you know, in the words of Greg Castanias, what makes them tick. They will see you as aligned with their goals. Again, rock star status.

Develop Business

The only thing better than making money off the firm's existing clients is helping the firm find new ones. Large law firms have full-time marketing and business development folks whose job is to give the firm leaders information about prospective client companies and help those leaders prepare to approach those companies about legal services. In other words, they help the firm make sales pitches.

Librarians, with their research skills, are the perfect complement to a firm's business development efforts. Your role can be to do the research (in a firm with no marketing staff) or to consult on business development by, say, recommending an appropriate database. LexisNexis, for example, has a tool called atVantage that you can use to:

- Get news, financial data, mergers and acquisitions activity, SEC and IP filings, and analytical reports on public and private companies

- See what types of lawsuits a company has been hit with and which firms are handling each lawsuit

- Create lists of prospects based on growth rate, profitability, geographic focus, or type of litigation

- Analyze long-term litigation trends and other marketplace factors[6]

This process of gathering information about a company, industry, or person, organizing and analyzing the results, and reporting on those results is called *competitive intelligence* (CI),[7] and law firms are doing it in a big way. In one 2009 survey, members of the NLJ 250 (the *National Law Journal* ranking of the 250-largest U.S. law firms) were asked how their firms are approaching CI. Seventy-seven firms responded, with the following results:

- Seventy-five percent are performing some type of CI, with another 9 percent in the planning phase.

- Twelve percent have a formal CI program.

- Thirty-nine percent of the total respondents have management or executive committee endorsement for CI activities.

- Sixty-two percent are seeing the CI requests increasing, 8 percent see them decreasing, and 28 percent report them staying the same.

- Twenty-four percent are seeing funding for CI increasing, 8 percent see it decreasing, and 55 percent report it staying the same.

- Forty-nine percent of those doing CI research report to the library, with the rest reporting to marketing teams, practice group leaders, or another firm department.[8]

Librarians, of course, are right in the middle of these CI efforts, and if they're not, they should be. In a 2009 article, Margaret Krause explains how this ambition might be accomplished:

> The Society of Competitive Intelligence Professionals (SCIP) claims its members have backgrounds in market research, government intelligence, or science and technology, but more and more librarians are clamoring for the opportunity to actually engage in competitive intelligence activities. Just look at the recent programs presented at the 2009 American Association of Law Libraries Annual Meeting. Law firm librarians are joining forces with the marketing department to produce trend analysis on emerging litigation, as well as intelligence on prospective clients and new hires. CI professionals can also monitor mergers and acquisitions, study the legal environment of a prospective location,

track emerging practice areas or identify a specific locale for an expanding law school.

Librarians need to be proactive in identifying ways to use competitive intelligence as a cost savings method for their patrons. As the organization's chief information professionals, librarians must be conversant about CI when meeting with their superiors. CI need not be a costly venture today with the prevalence of valuable information available at your fingertips. A little bit of forethought, curiosity, and persistence can uncover a goldmine of information, while keeping database expenditures to a minimum.[9]

Library Boards

As I mentioned earlier, county public libraries are overseen by boards of trustees. Some public law libraries are branches of county systems. Others are stand-alone, but if they are nonprofit entities, as most are, then they are led by volunteer trustees. Even court system libraries may be governed, or at least advised, by boards of trustees. An example is the New York State Unified Court System. Each county is required by statute to have a court law library, and each library must have a four-member board of trustees chaired by "a justice of the supreme court or, if no justice resides in the county, a judge of the county court, family court or of the surrogate's court of the county." The remaining three members must be an attorney, a county legislator, and someone recommended by the president of the county bar association (see N.Y. JUD. LAW § 814).

All nonprofit boards are similar in their organization, general responsibilities, and rules they must follow. An excellent discussion of nonprofits in general comes from the Authenticity Consulting Free Management Library (www.managementhelp.

org/boards/index.htm). Boards differ, of course, according to the character of the agencies they lead. How are library boards unique?

The boards of county public libraries tend to be wary of legal materials. They find them mysterious, know they are expensive, and are unsure how to manage them. Trustees also don't understand law library users. When the membership-based Mecklenburg County Law & Government Library, which I briefly managed, was in financial straits and beseeched Mecklenburg County to buy it out (see Chapter 10 for this story), one of the county trustees, a lawyer, told me the biggest hurdle was convincing the other trustees that "the library isn't just for lawyers" (see Chapter 3 for public use of law libraries). Public library boards are also scared to death of the unauthorized practice of law (see Chapter 3). I have worked with public librarians who would do little more than refer patrons with legal questions to other agencies. The fallacy of this approach is one of the reasons why I wrote *The Accidental Law Librarian*.

So how can a law librarian have a good relationship with trustees? First, think about why people volunteer for library boards in the first place: They love libraries. Specifically, they love *that* library, and they take pride in its success. If you do your part to make the library successful, you will endear yourself to the board. Second, keep the board involved. Give them a purpose and something important to do. If you don't, they will find their own projects, which may be trivial or a waste of money. That does not mean, however, that you should mire them in the details of acquisitions, MARC record uploads, or shelf-reading. Instead, keep them focused on the big picture.

Sadly, public law libraries in 2012 constantly need to justify themselves. Crushing cost increases and the perception that "everything is online" have weakened law libraries' status. How can you demonstrate your value to a board of trustees?

1. Cut, cut, cut costs. Then cut some more.

2. Be willing to consider *any* publication for cancellation. Trustees don't like to hear that a certain title is too valuable to lose when they never see anyone using it.

3. Get powerful lawyers (not just any lawyer) in town to advocate for you. They may not use the library often, but most lawyers, I have found, agree with the need for libraries *in principle*.

4. Get judges to advocate for you. Judges are gods in the legal world, and if enough judges think you're valuable, then you aren't going anywhere.

5. Partner with other city or county agencies (see Chapter 10 for examples).

6. Get a grant or two, and don't just look at the typical library grant sources. Also look at attorney organizations, especially the foundation of your state or local bar association. These groups usually fund projects intended to enhance public awareness and knowledge of the law or to better serve pro se users of the court system. It should be easy for a law library to design a project around such objectives.

For more information on library boards, I recommend Mary Y. Moore, *The Successful Library Trustee Handbook*, Second Edition (American Library Association, 2009). Written for prospective trustees, it discusses advocacy, strategic planning, policy development, fundraising, hiring and firing a director, and, interestingly, the future of libraries.

As librarians, we know, or think we know, where libraries are headed, but our trustees are not versed in the issues. They need us to educate them. This is the most important duty of a law librarian. Why? Your trustees will constantly be called upon to defend the library from those who want to chip away at its funding. You *must* make them experts in why this cannot occur. Don't give them propaganda, though; give them facts. Facts are an advocate's best ammunition.

Marketing the Law Library

Usually, library marketing means distributing flyers, inviting authors for book signings, and hosting game nights and stitch-ins and other activities. Throw in a summer reading program for kids, and you're on your way to bringing in more patrons, checking out more books, and answering more reference questions.

These are the measures of success for public libraries, and perhaps for public law libraries. Chapter 10 discusses some other ways to market a public law library. As I have said, however, most of these statistics mean nothing in a law firm. Attorneys do not have to visit the library to use its resources, and they definitely don't have to check out books. Even in a public law library, many of the materials do not circulate. How can you make the law firm library—and, more important, yourself as the librarian—integral to the firm's business? How can you make it—and you—indispensable?

1. Be a jack-of-all-trades. At various firms, I witnessed wills, helped with briefs, proofread annual reports, did client research, managed client extranets, and even helped in the mail room.

2. Form a good relationship with the office administrator. Preston, the administrator who set me straight about the politics of working with Gabriel, had been at the firm a long time. He knew what all the attorneys were doing and often steered them my way when he thought my abilities were well-suited for their particular projects.

3. Learn in detail what type of work each attorney does. Then recommend new websites, books, databases, and

other resources to those attorneys. Don't just send them a web link, however; explain why they need the resource. For a database, for example, arrange for free 30-day access and *show* the attorney how to use it.

4. Come up with a new business idea and write a proposal to present to upper management.

Writing a Business Proposal

Formal business proposals, also called business cases, are sometimes the best way to present your ideas to firm administrators or library boards. Several resources exist to help you with this:

- Gerald J. Alred, Charles T. Brusaw, and Walter E. Oliu, *The Business Writer's Handbook*, 10th ed. (Bedford/St. Martin's, 2011): Nearly 400 alphabetical entries on every aspect of workplace writing.

- Ulla de Stricker, *Business Cases for Info Pros: Here's Why, Here's How* (Information Today, 2008): The only business writing book available that is specifically for library professionals.

- Purdue Online Writing Lab (owl.english.purdue.edu): One of the best writing guides on the entire internet, containing more than 30 modules on professional and technical writing, including the 24-page "Planning and Organizing Proposals and Technical Reports" (owl. english.purdue.edu/media/pdf/20080628094326_727.pdf).

- Writing a Business Case, Strategic Librarian blog (www.strategiclibrarian.com/2007/10/18/writing-a-business-case): One of the few blogs dedicated to law firm librarianship, discussing seven components of a business case using library-related examples.

I wrote a business case in 2003, when I was the librarian for a corporate law department. We had begun a major effort to cut costs. In particular, we wanted to reduce the nearly $100 million per year we paid to outside law firms. Everyone had been asked to contribute cost-cutting ideas, and since my field was legal research, I came up with the idea of using specialized research and writing vendors to replace some of the work we outsourced to law firms. Encouraged by my boss, I wrote a business case and discussed it informally with several key people, all of whom seemed supportive. My intention was to then present it formally at a meeting of law department senior management.

Unfortunately, I was laid off before I could implement my ideas. Still, the business case raised my profile in the department. I have reproduced it as Appendix B. Written in 2003, it is a little dated, but it still offers insights into the workings of a corporate law department. More important, it is the type of work law librarians will have to consider to stay viable and prove themselves worthy members of an organization.

Endnotes

1. Katherine Rosin, "Success by the Book," *Legal Management* (May/June 2006): 65.
2. Ibid.
3. New York Public Library, "NYPL's Mission Statement," accessed November 27, 2012, www.nypl.org/help/about-nypl/mission.
4. University of San Francisco School of Law, "Dorraine Zief Law Library," accessed November 27, 2012, www.usfca.edu/law/library.
5. Greg Castanias, "How Librarians Add Value to Their Law Firms—Advice from Greg Castanias, Jones Day Library Partner," On Firmer Ground (blog), August 3, 2011, accessed November 27, 2012, www.firmerground.wordpress.com/2011/08/03/how-librarians-add-value-to-their-law-firms-advice-from-greg-castanias-jones-day-library-partner.
6. LexisNexis, "atVantage: Legal Prospects," accessed November 27, 2012, www.lexisnexis.com/intelligence/atvantage.page.

7. Camille Reynolds, Karen Hison, Kathy Skinner, and Nina Platt, "The Library as a Business Development, Competitive Intelligence and Client Relations Asset for Law Firms," American Association of Law Libraries, accessed November 27, 2012, www.aallnet.org/main-menu/Publications/products/Law-Librarians-Making-Information-Work/pll-guide-7.pdf.

8. Nina Platt, "Competitive Intelligence in Law Firms Survey Results," Strategic Librarian, August 21, 2009, accessed November 27, 2012, www.strategiclibrarian.com/2009/08/21/competitive-intelligence-in-law-firms-survey-results.

9. Margaret Krause, "Using Competitive Intelligence to Your Economic Advantage," *Law Library Lights* 53, no. 1 (Fall 2009): 1.

Chapter 9

Education and Resources

Outside academe, people thrust into the position of law librarian often have no background in the field of law. That was true of me when I started: I had an MLS, but no JD. Sometimes, however, law librarians start out as paralegals, file clerks, secretaries, or other professionals in the legal field but are rerouted into librarianship without the training (or, perhaps, the desire) to be librarians. I encountered that situation at Haynsworth Sinkler Boyd, and again a year later, when I took over a corporate law department library that had been under the reluctant stewardship of an accounting technician.

The value of a JD for law librarians is an ongoing debate, as is the value of another degree: the MBA. Most law firm and public law librarians lack both of these degrees. How are they successful? By taking advantage of the books, training opportunities, and professional support available to law librarians.

Should You Get a JD?

In the law librarian ejournal LLRX.com, George Butterfield wrote the definitive answer to this question.[1] Another excellent piece is Stephen Young's essay "The Dual Degree: A Requirement in Search of a Justification."[2] Following are my thoughts, which begin with a story.

When I worked at Charlotte School of Law, an instructor who taught first-year legal research and writing—we called it lawyering process, or LP—wanted me to help her create a new LP assignment. Claudia (not her real name) planned to give all the students the same set of facts and split them into plaintiffs and defendants. Each student would write an appellate brief for his or her side and, at semester's end, argue the case before a panel of "judges" consisting of LP faculty. The students would also be given the cases, statutes, and other authorities needed to write their briefs. The LP program had been using the same assignment for the previous 3 years, but now each instructor had been given the freedom to develop his or her own assignment. Claudia needed me to find authorities to support the new assignment she would be writing.

The old assignment had involved a teenage girl suing her high school because she was not allowed to join the wrestling team. This was a classic Title IX[3] case. Claudia wanted to keep the case school-centered but change it from a federal matter to a state one. She was interested in cases where a student was suspended for the length of his hair and sued the school on constitutional grounds. We discussed various indignities—a student suspended over his hair length, or having a tattoo, or using a cell phone—that have resulted in actual litigation. But those cases were all First Amendment claims (i.e., challenges to personal liberty). As a rule, first-year students have not studied constitutional law, so those scenarios wouldn't work.

Then Claudia had an idea. What if a student did something not to get suspended, but to lose a college scholarship? Not getting the scholarship might mean not going to college, which would mean not becoming a doctor, lawyer, or other high-wage earner. In other words, what if the high school unfairly deprived a student of the chance to start a career? The legal term for this is *interference*, which can be negligent (accidental) or tortious[4] (intentional). Each type can be further classified as interference with a contract or with a business relationship.

The four types of interference are *not* interchangeable, meaning that if you sue for tortious interference but the court finds that negligent interference occurred, you lose your suit. Why? You made the wrong accusation. Claudia decided the facts would suggest that the school had committed tortious interference with a business relationship by denying a student a scholarship. My job was to find actual North Carolina cases of this type.

You may assume, from my excellent overview of interference, that I understood the fine distinctions among the four types. I did not. The overview was cribbed from *North Carolina Torts*, second edition, by David and Wayne Logan. You may also assume that, using a keyword search on Westlaw (see Chapter 5), I had no trouble finding appropriate cases. Well, I did find cases containing the terms *tortious interference* and *business relationship*, but we could not use some of them. Why? There were different reasons. Maybe the case involved other elements besides interference and was decided on those elements. Or maybe it was not sufficiently analogous to the assignment. Claudia had to make those evaluations; my job was just to find the cases. This was a useful job for me to do. It saved Claudia time and prepared me for what would be my real job: being a resource for those students as they worked on their briefs. With a JD, though, I would have possessed the skill to find *and* evaluate the cases, freeing up Claudia to do something else. She would have bragged about the library staff to the entire faculty, a critical piece of library marketing (see Chapter 8).

A JD is an asset to a law firm librarian in the same way: It confers cachet and some expertise to make research projects a little smoother. For public law librarians, however, a JD is of little benefit—and can actually be a hindrance. Public patrons already ask for more help than librarians can legally (and practically) offer. If they knew a librarian had a law degree, they would be even likelier to ask for help drafting documents, interpreting statutes, and deciding case strategy. A public law librarian with a JD might be inclined to answer these questions, thus putting the library at risk. Law firms have malpractice insurance to pay the claim when legal advice goes awry, but public law libraries carry no such insurance.

Though I argue in Chapter 3 that legal reference rarely equals legal advice, a prudent law librarian always behaves as though that mis-understanding could occur. Having a JD makes that occurrence a little more likely.

There is one other way a JD will help a law librarian: advance-ment. In 2006, according to an article on Liscareer.com, "nearly six out of ten (55.6 percent) law librarians had earned an MLS without a JD. Another 24 percent had both degrees."[5] This statement com-bines academic with law firm and public law librarians. In aca-deme, the percentage with both degrees is higher. In law firms and public libraries, it is lower, even among managers. Why? Library boards and law firm administrators seem to recognize that legal skill is just one element of being a good law librarian. The total package of skills will earn a librarian a promotion, JD or not. By the same token, if only one candidate out of several has a JD, I have no doubt that, all other qualifications being equal, the JD candidate will win the job.

In academic law libraries, the JD is mandatory for moving up, at least at an American Bar Association–approved law school. ABA Standard 603(c) states, "A director of a law library should have a law degree and a degree in library or information science and shall have a sound knowledge of and experience in library administra-tion."[6] Although the standard says "should" and not "must," and you could argue that management, unlike reference work, requires little expertise in the law,[7] the chances of being a law school library director, or even a department head, without a JD are slim. Two reasons for this: 1) All the deans and faculty have JDs and will want the library managers to have them as well, and 2) library managers almost always have tenure-track faculty appointments, for which a JD is essential.

Some universities have combined JD and MLS programs,[8] allowing you to earn both degrees at once. I recommend this if you are thinking of library school and you *know* you want to be a law librarian. For those already in the field who want the JD, there are two options: Quit your job to go to law school full-time (unlikely) or keep working and get the degree part-time. Understand, however, that many law schools do not have part-time programs. Why? These schools view part-time degrees, and those who earn them, as inferior—and a lot of attorneys feel this way as well. Moreover, a part-time degree takes 4 or 5 years to complete. That is half a decade of squeezing one of the world's most demanding graduate programs into your spare time.

How About an MBA?

In Chapter 3, I said that some law firm librarians do as much business research as legal research. They get questions such as: What is the gross national product? What were Microsoft's profits last year? Who is the CEO of Baker & Taylor (a private company, which is hard to research)? Can I get a copy of the most recent 10-K for General Motors? The prevalence of these types of questions seems to suggest that holding an MBA as a second degree would boost a law librarian's career. Is this true?

An MBA would be an asset in some instances. The largest law firms (i.e., those with 100 or more attorneys) are divided into practice groups that are, broadly speaking, one of two types: litigation or transactional. Recall from Chapter 7 that litigation attorneys are what we most often think of when we think of lawyers. They go to trials, write briefs, file and answer complaints, conduct depositions, and handle appeals. If their case is a business case—say, a company's shareholders suing the board of directors over misstated earnings—then they would need the type of business research mentioned previously. If, however, the case is a Clean Water Act suit, or an Americans with Disabilities Act claim, or a criminal defense, then MBA skills will likely not be needed.

Transactional attorneys would be the real consumers of these skills. Such lawyers negotiate contracts, buy or sell companies, apply for patents, set up limited liability companies (LLCs) or limited liability partnerships (LLPs), design an employer's compensation or employee benefits plan, or write the will that gives Blaydon Graycastle's entire estate to a bewitching blonde. An MBA-trained librarian, upon being asked for a company's 10-Q,[9] or that day's LIBOR,[10] or an example of a REIT[11]—all requests I have gotten and met with a *sotto voce* whimper—would no doubt know immediately what to do.

Yet I found all these things without an MBA. (So do most business librarians. According to various surveys, only about 20 percent hold this degree.[12]) How? I did a little research on the terminology before looking for the appropriate document. Or I simply asked the requesting attorney what it was. Business lawyers know their field is not widely understood, even by other lawyers, so they don't mind explaining a few concepts en route to getting the documents they need from a librarian.

Books on Law Librarianship

There aren't many other books on law librarianship beyond the classic I mentioned in the introduction, Deborah Panella and Ellis Mount's *Basics of Law Librarianship* (1991). By "classic," I mean "dreadfully old." So much has changed since this title (like, say, the internet) that, as an introductory text, it is only slightly useful.

Some more recent general works include:

Law Librarianship in the Twenty-First Century (2006, Scarecrow Press), edited by Roy Balleste, Sonia Luma-Lamas, and Lisa Smith-Butler

This book aims to be comprehensive, with chapters on public services, collection development and acquisitions, government documents, administration, technology, law library history, and more. Once you get past the preponderance of prolegomena—foreword by University of South Florida library science professor Vicki Gregory; preface and acknowledgements by the editors; and an introduction by Roy Mersky, law librarianship's *éminencegrise*—you see that, except for Chapter 2, "Working at the Law Library: A Practical Guide," and a page in Chapter 8 on case management software, the book mostly applies to academic libraries. For example, Chapter 3, "Administration," offers advice on working with a law school dean but not a law firm managing partner. No one outside a university would know or care about microforms, print indexes, faculty status, CALI, or ABA accreditation. And despite the growing globalization of legal practice, less than a baker's dozen of American law firm librarians would get any benefit from this book's discussion of foreign, comparative, and international law librarianship.

For those, however, who see in law librarianship not just a job but a human drama, this book, like most academic writing, provides needed context. In the foreword, Gregory observes that law librarianship "has been treated as a stepchild" for years by library science professors. Now, though, "electronic storage of documents, Boolean searching methods, and the steady evolution away from reliance on print resources … have served to make law librarianship today a branch of 21st-century librarianship rather than a branch of the study and practice of law." Kinda makes you feel proud, doesn't it?

Public Services in Law Libraries: Evolution and Innovation in the 21st Century, edited by Barbara Bintliff and Lee F. Peoples (2007, Haworth Information Press)

Let's see … two chapters on faculty services, one on student services, one on teaching students, and one on, of all things, services to law school administrative staff. Yet this book is not as law school–heavy as others. Law firms get a full chapter, as do state and county law libraries. Plus, there are chapters on privacy, marketing, and other topics that, while ostensibly about all libraries, apply more readily to those outside academe.

Something unique in this book is the chapter on online catalogs. OPAC discussions often appear in the wider library literature, but they are rare in the law library field. The chapter's theme is innovation. "Online retailers such as Amazon.com have raised the bar for the delivery of information," observe the authors, who also bring up Netflix, iTunes, LibraryThing, Facebook, and other snazzy sites that make an OPAC look pretty unfashionable. Legal research is a closed universe, and practitioners are familiar with most of the tools, so the catalog tends to be overlooked in law library usage. Big mistake, argue the authors of this chapter, who recommend ways not just to use the catalog more, but to use it better.

Law Library Collection Development in the Digital Age, edited by Michael G. Chiorazzi and Gordon Russell (2002, Haworth Information Press)

This is the first book-length treatment of collection development in law libraries. It was heralded when it came out as a first-rate work of scholarship that also addressed the everyday concerns of the working librarian. Very few of these concerns have changed in the 10 years since the book was published.

Westlaw and LexisNexis, the Ford and Chevy of legal databases, were just moving from CD-ROM to the internet in 2001, when this book was being written, so you can pretty much ignore its descriptions of the inner-workings of those databases. Also, unless you work in an academic law library, pay little attention to chapters such as Michael Chiorazzi's "Books, Bytes, Bricks and Bodies: Thinking about Collection Use in Academic Law Libraries." As I explained in Chapter 1, academic law libraries have a patron base

(professors) and collection priorities (interdisciplinary, comprehensive, and obscure) not shared by law firms or public libraries.

Other chapters, however, are timeless, such as John Detham's
chapter on the consolidation of legal publishing companies. The
decade since 2002 has seen more mergers, of course, but Detham's
background is essential for any law librarian. Ditto Scott
Matheson's chapter on access versus ownership. Again, today's
electronic products are way ahead of last decade's, but there are
still only two options for acquiring them: lease or buy. Matheson
details the considerations for each. Finally, Julie Turner's chapter
on electronic court records tackles a subject that rarely appears in
the law library literature. Yet searching court records is a huge part
of what law firm and public law librarians do every day.

The Changing Role of Law Firm Librarianship (2008, Aspatore
Books)

One of a few recent titles devoted to this topic (another is *How
to Manage a Law Firm Library*, also by Aspatore Books), this book
is a collection of essays by library managers of monolithic, sometimes multinational, law firms. The overall theme, as the title
implies, is change—in other words, how the duties and purpose of
the law librarian are changing as these huge firms are created by
the mergers and mercy-killings of smaller ones. As new librarians
don't know what the law firms are changing *from*, they will need to
use their imaginations, especially with passages such as "In the
mid-eighties … case law research meant the West digests or the
ALR annotation system. Case verification meant using a stack of
Shepards Citations." *Shepards*—is that a pie? Bit players at the
Nativity? (See Chapter 5 for a discussion of *Shepard's*, complete
with apostrophe.)

Clearly, this book was not written for novice librarians. With a little experience, however, you will find that most of it opens like a

spring tulip. You don't need the argot of law librarians to understand the main challenges facing today's law firm libraries, which are:

1. Rising cost of publications
2. Transition to electronic resources
3. Marketing the library
4. Staying relevant
5. Becoming beloved

I discuss other challenges in Chapter 10. To see these same challenges discussed by multiple authors reinforces to new librarians the importance of mastering the relevant skills. To see them discussed from multiple angles gives new librarians a head start in that mastering process.

None of the authors just noted, however, discusses what I think is the hardest skill to learn: understanding the attorney mindset. I touch on this in Chapters 3 and 8, but there is much, much more.

Books on Legal Research

Law librarianship, as I said earlier in this chapter, is about a lot more than legal research. Yet the librarian who fails to develop sharp research skills will soon be out of a job. The books on librarianship just mentioned discuss legal research in general—too general to be of much use. To get the needed expertise, you should read at least two of the following books dedicated to legal research: first one written for the layperson, then one written for a legal professional.

For laypersons:

- *Legal Research Made Easy*, fourth edition
  (SphinxLegal, 2005)

- *Legal Research: How to Find and Understand the Law,* 16th edition (Nolo Press, 2012)

For professionals:

- *Fundamentals of Legal Research*, ninth edition, Thomson West (2009)
- *Legal Research Methods,* second edition, Foundation Press (2009)
- *Legal Research and Writing for Paralegals*, sixth edition, Aspen (2011)

The layperson's books are self-help types of books. Why start with one of those? Because they are easier to understand. Self-help books don't cover everything law librarians need to know, however, which is why you need the professional book as well. Table 9.1 lists a few more distinctions between the two types.

Research Guides

Print

As you read in Chapter 2, each state has its own statutes, cases, and regulations that determine lawful or unlawful behavior in that state. There are also state-specific secondary sources, used all the time by attorneys in that state. For example, North Carolina has:

- *Strong's North Carolina Index* (an encyclopedia of North Carolina law)
- *North Carolina Contracts*
- *Brandis and Broun on North Carolina Evidence*

These are major titles used by most North Carolina attorneys. However, out-of-state attorneys and public patrons might not be familiar with them. Plus there are obscure titles, such as *North*

Table 9.1   Distinctions Between Self-Help and Professional Legal Titles

Layperson	Legal Professional
Help layperson conduct basic legal research.	Help legal professional become expert in research sources and methods.
Describe the basics of the American court system and legislative process.	Describe the court system and legislative process in more detail.
Cover the basics of researching statutes and cases.	In addition to statutes and cases, discuss administrative law, legislative history, and court rules and procedures.
Focus on the major secondary sources, such as legal encyclopedias.	Cover lesser-used secondary sources, such as legal periodicals and looseleaf services.
Do not discuss specialized areas of research.	Sometimes discuss specialized areas of research (e.g., tax and international law in Thomson West text).
May cover the basics of legal writing (e.g., Nolo book).*	Spend little time on legal writing (except for Aspen paralegal text).
Often include library exercises and hypothetical research problems *with solutions*.	Use Aspen text, which includes exercises but not solutions.

*As I explained in Chapter 3, law firm librarians can make themselves indispensible by proofreading the firm's work product, so some knowledge of legal writing is a boon. Plus, it helps your credibility with attorneys, especially more senior ones, to speak their language—*brief, complaint, answer, interrogatories*, and so on.

Carolina Real Property Mechanics' Liens, Future Advances, and Equity Lines, unknown even to most in-state practitioners.

As a law librarian, you might want to recommend any of these titles to a researcher, but how would you even know about them? Answer: *North Carolina Legal Research* (2010) by Scott Childs. It is one of several published bibliographies of North Carolina law. Comparable bibliographies, or research guides, exist for every state, often published by W.S. Hein (www.wshein.com), and you can find most of them at any academic law library. Just search the library catalog for *research guide* and the state you're interested in.

There are also guides for other countries and even for specific areas of law. These are useful not just for identifying monographs and treatises—a good catalog search will find those—but for journal articles, major statutes and cases, administrative rulings (hard to identify otherwise), or just the structure of another country's legal system. Some examples are:

- *Legal Ethics: A Legal Research Guide* (W.S. Hein, 2006)

- *Federal Tax Research: Guide to Materials and Techniques* (Foundation Press, 2007)

- *Guide to International Legal Research* (Butterworths, 2010)

- *A Guide to European Union Law* (Sweet & Maxwell, 2007)

- *Statutes Compared: A U.S., Canadian Research Guide to Statutes by Subject* (W.S. Hein, 2001)

Online

In addition to print research guides, most academic law libraries have electronic guides posted on their websites. These tend to be less in-depth than print guides, covering only the major resources familiar to practitioners. Some go beyond the basics, however, listing, for example, specific Westlaw and LexisNexis databases on certain subjects. Plus, online guides are updated more frequently than the hard copies. Three of the best are those from the Georgetown Law Library, the University of Washington Gallagher Law Library, and the Cornell University Law Library.

The Georgetown Law Library Research Guides listing (www.ll.georgetown.edu/research) comprises over 100 topical guides (Figure 9.1), including non-U.S. law guides—United Nations, European Union, treaties, international agreements—not found at most law libraries. The guide also includes self-paced online tutorials ideal for *seeing* the research process (as opposed to reading about it in one of the previously mentioned books).

The Legal Research Guides from the Gallagher Law Library at the University of Washington (lib.law.washington.edu/ref/guides. html) consist of hundreds of guides indexed by topic rather than listed alphabetically like Georgetown's guides (Figure 9.2). Many are on new areas of concern—blogs/RSS feeds, genetics, end-of-life issues—and there are several on careers, an old concern dressed in new hardships. Washington's MLS program has *the* best

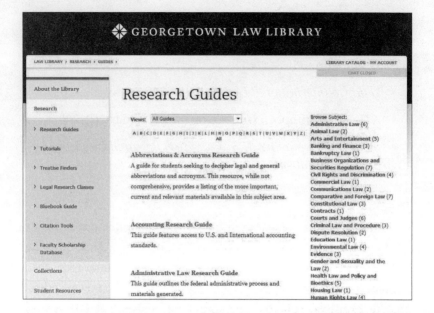

Figure 9.1　Georgetown Law Library Research Guides

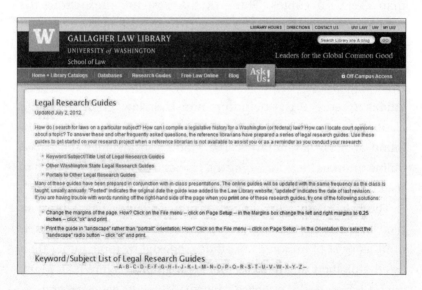

Figure 9.2　Gallagher Law Library's Legal Research Guides

law librarian track in the country, which is reflected in the guides catering to librarian concerns—Bluebook 101, Legal Dictionaries, Going Beyond Casebooks. The best guide on the site? Judicial Humor. Go there and read it now.

The Legal Research Engine from Cornell University Law Library (www.lawschool.cornell.edu/library/WhatWeDo/ResearchGuides /CLL-Legal-Research-Engine.cfm) is a simple-interface search engine for research guides, legal blogs, and other law-related websites (Figure 9.3).

Blawgs

Blawgs are law-related blogs. These can be great sources for news, trends, opinions, and professional development. Several good ones specific to law librarians[13] are discussed here.

LLRX.com (www.llrx.com) is a monthly ejournal whose editor, Sabrina Pacifici, has a corresponding blog, beSpacific (www.be spacific.com). LLRX, which stands for Law Librarian Resource Exchange, is simply *the best* law librarian site out there. Why? It includes thousands of original articles, dating back to the 1990s, on *exactly* what law librarians need to know (Figure 9.4). Some examples are:

- "Digging for Clues About Public Companies"
- "Development of a SharePoint Site"
- "Deal or No Deal: Licensing and Acquiring Digital Resources"
- "Marketing Yourself with Webinars"
- "Using the Kindle in Library Settings"

The Law Librarian Blog (www.lawprofessors.typepad.com/ law_librarian_blog) is a traditional blog (Figure 9.5), with news

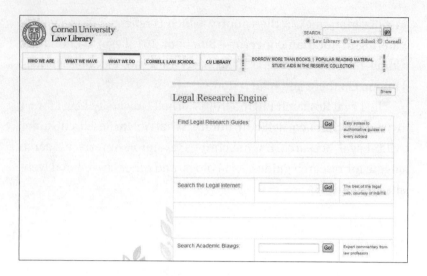

Figure 9.3   Cornell University Law Library's Legal Research Engine

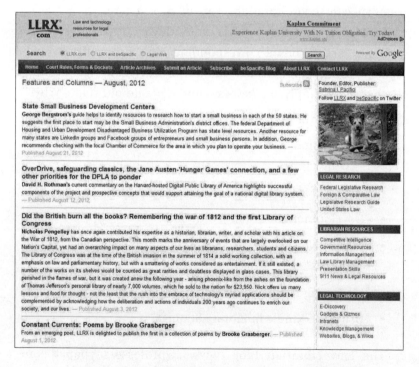

Figure 9.4   Features and Columns section of LLRX.com

Figure 9.5   Postings on the Law Librarian Blog

("Baltimore Law Budget Increase Raises Some Questions"), job postings, commentary, case summaries, blog links, tense humor, and five-minutes-I'll-never-get-back weirdness (see "Friday Fun: Lego Law for *Palsgraf v. Long Island Railroad*," October 21, 2011). Some pieces, though, are invaluable professionally, such as "Some Thoughts on Thomson's Acquisition of West Being Honored as Worst Legal Publishing Merger" (October 24, 2011).

OK, I list this one for a selfish reason: The Charlotte Law Library News (www.charlottelawlibrary.wordpress.com) was co-founded by me when I worked at Charlotte School of Law. Back then, we posted once a month and averaged three hits a day (two of them were me, inflating the stats). Now it is updated daily, tricked out with surveys and pictures, and able to be shared on Facebook, Twitter, Digg, Reddit, LinkedIn, and Lord knows where else (Figure 9.6). Many of the posts are adverts for the library, but some—Mary Susan Lucas's article on finding North Carolina

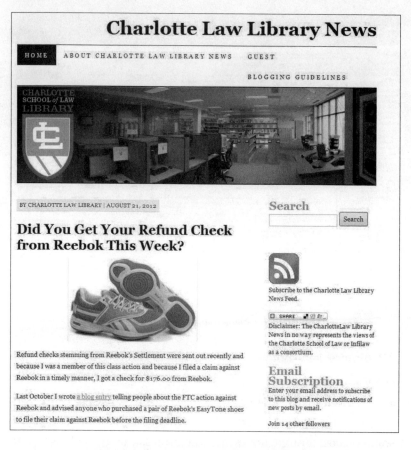

Figure 9.6 Charlotte Law Library News homepage

forms, for example—are useful to any librarian. Oh, and make sure you check out the original comic strip, *Murphy's Law School*, written by yours truly and drawn by librarian Kim Allman.

Law Library Blogs (www.aallcssis.pbworks.com/w/page/1189465/Law-Library-Blogs) provides an alphabetical list of more than 200 law librarian blogs, each with the name of its host institution, and is updated once or twice a month (Figure 9.7).

It is also worth your time to read attorney blogs—you will learn more about legal subjects and the practice of law, making you a more valuable law librarian. At the Top 100 Law and Lawyer Blogs (www.criminaljusticedegreesguide.com/library/the-top-100-law-and-lawyer-blogs.html), blogs are ranked within each of several categories: General Law, Law Professors, Law Students, Judiciary, Criminal Law, Corporate Law, Employment Law, Real Estate Law, Internet and Cyber Law, Environmental Law, Foreign Law, Legal Ethics, and Law Office Technology (Figure 9.8).

Training and Support

As I explained in Chapter 4, you will use Westlaw or LexisNexis for 75–80 percent of your research, so it is crucial to become an expert on them. The best way to do this is to take advantage of the abundant free training West and Lexis will offer you.

Westlaw User Guides

All Westlaw guides (www.store.westlaw.com/support/user-guide/westlaw/default.aspx) are full-color PDF files that can be printed or saved to your computer. The main guides consist of four categories:

- Westlaw Basics: Signing on, navigation, retrieving cases and statutes, and other essentials
- Westlaw by Practice Area: More than 20 specific practice areas covered
- Westlaw for your Organization: Law firms, corporations, governments, or law schools (check out Cost-Effective Research Tips under Managing Your Westlaw Account)
- Alternative Access Methods: Public, college, prison, and other nonlaw libraries

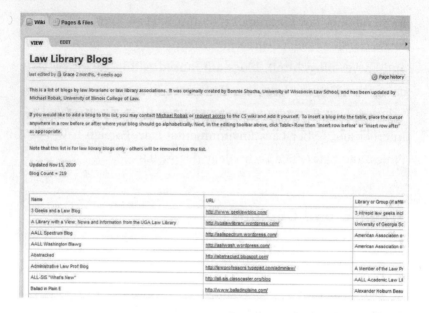

Figure 9.7   Law Library Blogs homepage

Figure 9.8   Top 100 Law and Lawyer Blogs homepage

There are also guides for WestlawNext, the newest offshoot of Westlaw (see Chapter 4), as well as other general technical and research support.

Westlaw Training

How do you want it—telephone, in-person, or self-paced? West offers all these options for Westlaw Training (www.store.westlaw.com/support/training/default.aspx). Telephone and in-person training are the best, but these have limits. West won't pay someone to travel to your library once a week, of course, and the telephone trainers do have thousands of other clients to support.

Not to worry: The self-paced webinars are fantastic, too. For example, solo and small law firms can choose from 54 webinars—36 for Westlaw, 18 for WestlawNext—each about 30 minutes long. That is *27 hours* of free Westlaw training. From there, you can move to the Government and Education and the Corporate and Nonprofit webinars, each giving you a different perspective on how a particular type of attorney uses Westlaw.

Westlaw Librarian Resource Center

The user guides and training options found in the Westlaw Librarian Resource Center (www.store.westlaw.com/support/librarian/default.aspx) were created with attorneys and paralegals in mind. West, however, understands the different needs of librarians, employing a Library Relations Team to meet those needs. These folks are librarians, not attorneys or salespeople; they know the pressures and problems you're facing, and they want to help you solve these problems—using Westlaw, of course.

The best way to use the Library Relations Team is as consultants for specific projects you're working on. The website, however, has some good general resources:

- PowerPoint presentations (e.g., The Impact of Globalization on IP Research)

- Wolf v. Pig (the *best* way to learn the topic and key number system)

- Webinars (litigation resources, law firm profitability, expert witness research, and more)

- Several newsletters (*Law Librarians in the New Millennium* is a good one)

LexisNexis User Guides

LexisNexis User Guides (www.lexisnexis.com/literature/default. asp) can be found under Product Literature, and there are only nine of them—far fewer than West provides. Learning Lexis.com, however, is 40 pages long, and it covers the details of signing in, searching and viewing results, topics and headnotes (*not* the same as Westlaw topics and key numbers), Shepardizing, and special Lexis products such as Total Litigator and Transactional Advisor.

LexisNexis Training

Like Westlaw, Lexis has telephone, on-site, and webinar training (www.lexisnexis.com/custserv/Training). One unique program is the Paralegal Mastery Program, consisting of five telephonic modules of about an hour each. The modules are:

- Initial Case Analysis

- Cite Checking With *Shepard's*

- Drafting Legal Documents

- Public Records and News

- Company and Financial Information

I completed these five modules early in my career and earned a certificate, which still hangs in my office. More important, I gained some paralegal-level skills, which have helped me at every stage of my career.

LexisNexis InfoPro

Lexis has catered to librarians longer than West, and it shows on the LexisNexis InfoPro website (www.law.lexisnexis.com/infopro), a rich collection of resources in six categories. Some of the resources are:

- Keeping Current: Two newsletters, as well as new sources and other changes

- Training and Resources: Links to one of the best law librarian resources of any type, Zimmerman's Research Guide

- Literature and Reference Materials: All the user guides *not* posted under Product Literature, plus case studies, white papers (e.g., "Top Five Attributes of a Reliable Public Records Search"), and other resources

- Professional and Personal Development: Especially Promoting Your Library, which is not so much professional development as professional survival

- Librarian Relations Group: Fabulous team of consultants, accessible at no charge

- Corporate InfoPro Resources: Corporate and business resources that law librarians also need to know

Associations

American Association of Law Libraries

The American Association of Law Libraries (AALL; www.aall.org) is the premier professional association for law librarians. Early in my career, someone told me *not* to join AALL, hinting that it was a bunch of snobs and I wouldn't get anything out of it. This was terrible advice! When I joined years later, I found the members to be smart and helpful, the annual meetings to be fun and educational, and the website to be chock-full of information. Their top three website resources are:

- AALL2go (www.softconference.com/aall): Webinars, annual meeting recordings, and handouts on a variety of topics including library management, teaching, information technology, reference, and more

- Biennial Salary Survey: Comparative salary information for law librarians broken out by position, region, education, years in current position, and years of library experience

- Special Interest Sections: Membership subgroups that usually maintain their own websites with newsletters, web links, and other information

AALL.org also links to 31 regional chapter websites. The chapter sites are useful for the local links and information they provide. The best is the Washington, DC chapter (www.llsdc.org) for its *Legislative Source Book*, a clearinghouse of U.S. and state legislative and regulatory information.

Special Libraries Association

Though it caters to business and corporate librarians, the Special Libraries Association (SLA; www.sla.org) is concerned with some topics that cross over to law librarianship. The Resources tab links to Information Portals, Industry Reports, and other research on topics such as copyright, electronic licensing, digital libraries, budgeting, benchmarking, knowledge management, user training, and dozens of other areas relevant to law librarians.

Through Click University (www.sla.org/content/learn), members can take free webinars or enroll in one of three premium programs: competitive intelligence, copyright management, or knowledge management. Consisting of eight to nine courses each, the programs are expensive—around $4,000—but in-depth. "There is no other equivalent existing educational opportunity available," claims the Click University website. Too true.

Endnotes

1. George Butterfield, "Is a JD Necessary for Law Librarians?"LLRX. com, June 25, 2007, accessed November 29, 2012, www.llrx.com/ features/jdnecessary.htm.
2. See Stephen Young, "The Dual Degree: A Requirement in Search of a Justification," *AALL Spectrum* 17, no. 3 (December 2012): 7–10.
3. As in, Title IX of the Education Amendments of 1972, stating that "[n]o person in the United States shall, on the basis of sex, be excluded from participation in, be denied the benefits of, or be subjected to discrimination under any education program or activity receiving Federal financial assistance." This law amended the 1964 Civil Rights Act.
4. *Tortious* means "pertaining to a tort" (i.e., a wrongful act). Do not confuse it with *torturous*, meaning "causing torture," or *tortuous*, meaning "twisting, winding." Wrongful acts can be akin to torture, however, and many of them are twisted, but never mind—I have already gotten lost in this winding note.
5. Amy Burchfield, "Experience the World as an FCIL Librarian," LISCareer.com, June 2006, accessed November 29, 2012, www.lis career.com/burchfield_fcil.htm.
6. *2011–2012 Standards and Rules of Procedure for Approval of Law Schools*, ABA Section of Legal Education and Admissions to the Bar, accessed November 29, 2012, www.americanbar.org/groups/legal_ education/resources/standards.html.
7. Young, "The Dual Degree," 7–8.
8. A list of these is available at www.aallnet.org/main-menu/Careers/ lawlibrarycareers/Education-Requirements/state.html.
9. *10-Q* refers to a company's quarterly report, filed every 3 months with the SEC.
10. *LIBOR* means London Interbank Offered Rate, the rate at which the world's most preferred borrowers are able to borrow money.
11. *REIT* stands for Real Estate Investment Trust, which is like a mutual fund for real estate.

12. Young, "The Dual Degree," 8.
13. See Lisa Smith-Butler, "Cost Effective Legal Research Redux: How to Avoid Becoming the Accidental Tourist, Lost in Cyberspace," *Florida Coastal Law Review* 9, no. 3 (Spring 2008): 293–346.

Chapter 10

The Future of Law Libraries

After law libraries as we know them first began appearing in the mid-19th century, they looked and operated with little change for nearly 150 years. Then came the 1990s. Since then, public and private law libraries have undergone a revolution that the profession is still trying to understand. What does the future hold for law libraries? How will their collections and users continue to change? The last few years have seen many law libraries close their doors amid budgetary bloodlettings. How can the law library as an institution survive?

Resources

As you saw in Chapter 1, prices for law-related publications have exploded in recent years. Expect that trend to continue, especially as more and more libraries cancel their print subscriptions in the face of budget stagnation or outright cuts. Consolidation among legal publishers has created the Big Three (see Chapter 1), and while consolidation ensures some revenue growth, that growth will not keep pace with print cancellations. At some point, the Big Three must consider silencing the presses on some of their oldest but least-used print titles, such as digests and case reporters (West), *Shepard's Citations* (Lexis), and Common Clearing House looseleaf services (WoltersKluwer). Treatises and practice guides, however, especially those focused on one jurisdiction or covering an emerging area of law, will continue to be published and used in print format.

One way that West has tried to help libraries manage costs is through library maintenance agreements, which guarantee a limit on price increases in exchange for the library's promise to maintain its subscriptions. The idea is a good one, though most librarians have been dissatisfied with West's implementation.[1] Expect other publishers to perfect this idea or to develop their own contractual innovations.

As publishers retrench on print materials, they are going ahead full tilt on electronic ones. Lexis, West, Hein, and other vendors are deepening their mainstream databases, and they are also creating new products such as WestlawNext and Lexis Advance. These new interfaces use Google-like technology to make searching easier. Vendors are also creating apps for cell phones, tablets, and other mobile devices (see Chapter 6), which are always becoming more widespread and sophisticated.

Like commercial vendors, university law journals are also taking advantage of the economies of electronic publication. More than 400 full-text journals are available through the ABA Free Full-Text Online Law Review/Journal Search (www.americanbar.org/groups/ departments_offices/legal_technology_resources/resources/free_ journal_search.html), which has an oafish name but sweet functionality. Powered by Google, the site searches the articles on all the member journal websites. The online articles would include only those published in the last few years, so for older issues, you would still need Westlaw, LexisNexis, or HeinOnline. However, the database is growing fast: Between 2010 and 2012, it went from 350 journals to over 400.[2]

Arguments over print versus electronic publication of law journals have grown more heated in recent years thanks to the Durham Statement, a 2009 manifesto written at Duke University in Durham, North Carolina. The statement called for law schools to provide access to their journals in "stable, open, digital formats" and to stop publishing them in print.[3] This second demand set off a controversy within the law librarian community. Its proponents complain that hard-copy journals are expensive to print, mail, buy, and store. New issues are already digitized on Westlaw, LexisNexis, and HeinOnline, so why keep printing them? Detractors point to the word "stable" in the manifesto, arguing that no other format is as stable as print.

To me, stability is not those detractors' real gripe. Their real gripe is the death of print, which is ironic. Law librarians routinely chuckle at living-in-the-past attorneys who insist on keeping print reporters and digests. Yet here is a subset of the librarians doing the same with a secondary source, one that is not superior in print format. For now, the print enthusiasts win because the legal field isn't ready for a major law journal to suspend physical production. Eventually, though, one of them will take this step. Ironically, it will most likely be one—Harvard, Yale, Columbia, Duke, etc.—that does not need the cost savings. Its motive will be to start a trend, and in the copycat world of law schools, that is what will happen. Within a decade, most of the other journals will have followed its lead.

Attorneys will always need law journals for reflection and analysis. But for news on legal developments—a role once played by law journals—they are turning to noncommercial outlets such as blogs (see Chapter 9 for blog finding aids). The so-called open law movement has also given us more providers of free primary sources. FindLaw and LexisOne (now LexisNexis Communities) were among the first, and they had their limitations: FindLaw had no search engine and didn't include any federal district cases, while LexisOne went back only 10 years for all jurisdictions except the U.S. Supreme Court. Newer sites include Public Library of Law (www.plol.org), Justia (www.justia.com), and Google Scholar (www.scholar.google.com).

A latecomer to the legal industry, Google has immediately become a major player due to its trademark search engine, which

West and Lexis have emulated with WestlawNext and Lexis Advance. It has already squeezed out one competitor, AltLaw.org. "While we could see [Google] as the 800-pound gorilla stomping on our pet project," read a farewell message on the AltLaw homepage, "the truth is that we—a small academic group within Columbia Law School—were never really equipped to handle the challenges of building and maintaining a state-of-the-art search engine." Look for Google to expand its coverage until it rivals PLOL, Justia, and other free providers.

In fact, look for *more* free providers as part of an expansion of the open law movement. Carl Malamud, founder of Public. Resource.Org (see Chapter 6), isn't going away. In addition to digitizing the *Federal Reporter,* his foundation is working with numerous federal and state agencies on digitization and accesss projects. In a 2010 interview with *Library Journal,* he says "[a]ccess to the law in particular in the United States is a $10 billion a year industry, and it's a very inequitable system in which government lawyers and solo practitioners and a lot of different groups don't have the same access to the legal materials that those who are more well heeled have."[4]

That is not true, of course. Most government lawyers and solo practitioners subscribe to Westlaw, LexisNexis, Fastcase, or one of the other alternatives. The coverage is smaller than that of large firms, but the small entities are not lacking government information—cases, statutes, and regulations. Even the scantiest subscriptions include these. What they are missing are secondary sources—encyclopedias, treatises, journals, magazines, newspapers, newsletters, and other commercial publications. These are what you pay for when you pay for Wexis.

You also pay for easy access. Malamud calls access to knowledge "a universal human right," going on to say that "[o]ur copyright laws are clear that works of the federal government shall be public domain."[5] Well, yeah. Westlaw and LexisNexis do nothing to alter information's public domain-ness. If an attorney wanted to, on her own, obtain every opinion from every American court every day of her career, organizing and storing the opinions in a way to make retrieval efficient, she would be free to do so. Or she can pay for this service, and do what she does best—represent clients—and leave the storage and retrieval to the specialists.

To me, *information* is the universal human right, not knowledge. Information is cloth; knowledge is clothing. One becomes the other through desire and hard work, which are not mandates. To make knowledge is to make meaning, and there is nothing universal about that: Each person's meaning is *sui generis*. The materials, the information, are and should be free, but how many of us can make meaning from them? We pay others to assemble all sorts of consumer goods, so I don't see the antidemocracy of paying others to organize information.

Still, the open law movement is here to stay, and I see it growing, especially with librarian support. Joe Hodnicki, editor of the invaluable Law Librarian Blog (see Chapter 9), wrote a series of companionable articles on the open law movement in 2009–2010, which are available on the Future of Law Libraries wiki (www. cyber.law.harvard.edu/futurelawlib/Main_Page) along with other suggested readings.

Users

I teach freshman English at a college part-time. As part of my students' library orientation, I have them do a scavenger hunt. One of the questions is to tell me which pages of David Remnick's book *Lenin's Tomb* discuss Ronald Reagan. Easy, right? Just find the book in the stacks and look up *Reagan* in the index.

One student tried a different approach, one which I suppose was more natural to him. He called me over to the computer where he was sitting, pointed to the question, and said he wasn't sure how to find the answer. I saw he had typed into Google *what pages discuss ronald reagan in lenin's tomb by david remnick.*

Across America, 19-year-olds are making plans for law school, and when they get out in 2021 or so, who knows what the internet will make possible? However, they will still need print research skills because some things, *a lot* of things, will not exist electronically. Ebooks have flourished in the last few years, but it would take forever to digitize all the monographs back to the invention of the printing press. At my first law firm, an attorney asked me to find Theodore Roosevelt's senior thesis at Harvard, which I got a Harvard librarian to copy and fax to me. There is no guarantee that document will ever be digitized.

Similarly, many U.S. Congressional documents are online, but many more are not. The gap seems to be from 1969, when the *U.S. Serial Set* ceased publication, to the beginning of the World Wide Web in the mid-1990s. It was a crucial time period—the Vietnam War came to a close, Title VII was amended, and major environmental, immigration, and energy bills were passed—and its documents are frequently cited. Currently, the only way to get them is hard copy. Other resources that may never see the light of a scanner are:

- State and local bar journals
- Professional newsletters
- Non-U.S. publications
- Superseded statutes (you can get these on Westlaw or LexisNexis back to the mid-1990s, but for earlier ones, you will likely need ... wait for it ... *microfiche*)[6]

Librarians know the everything-is-online mentality to be a Google-fueled fiction. So do older attorneys, who shake their heads at the young associates' digital overreliance. "When I am researching in the library," writes Scott Stolley, a partner in a

Dallas, Texas, firm, "I feel as lonely as the Maytag repairman."[7] Stolley describes his policy of requiring associates who research for him to begin with books, a burden I saw in the eyes of summer law clerks who trudged into my office to ask for help because so-and-so "won't let me use Westlaw."

Of course, Luddites like Stolley will be gone someday, leaving the fate of law libraries in the hands of the Google generation. Some have already closed from lack of use. In 2008, Justice Sharon Lee of the Tennessee Supreme Court defended the decision to shutter three court libraries by saying, "We were not getting our money's worth out of it at all. Most of our research is online now."[8] In 2007, county commissioners in Miami voted to end the funding for the county's 70-year-old public law library.[9] Three years later, Indiana law librarian Zoya Golban turned off the lights and locked the doors at the Marion County Law Library for the last time.[10] Patrons thereafter would have to use the county library, which agreed to take a portion of the law library's collection. That same year, law libraries in the Connecticut towns of Milford, Willimantic, and Norwich were boarded up.[11]

One of the low points of my career was presiding over the closing of the Mecklenburg County Law & Government Library (MCL&GL) in Charlotte, North Carolina. MCL&GL had its roots in the Charlotte Law Library, a private membership library begun in the 1930s. Membership law libraries date back to the Law Library Company of Philadelphia, begun in 1802. Attorneys bought ownership in the collection at $20 per share, which enabled them to use the collection and "socialize with other prestigious members of the company."[12] The Charlotte Law Library had a similar structure. Members owned the collection and were the only ones with access to it.

But Charlotte, a growing city, needed a public law library, and by 1990, the attorney members needed help with the rising costs of library operation. Both goals were accomplished with a unique partnership between the law library and the Public Library of Charlotte & Mecklenburg County (PLCMC). The members would continue to own and pay for the collection, while the public library would provide full-time staff members, computer support, and other administrative needs. The renamed Mecklenburg County Law & Government Library would relocate to an unused county building and, in exchange for paying no rent, allow public access 9–5 on weekdays. Member access would be 24/7 and controlled by electronic key cards given to each member. Members would also retain their borrowing privileges.[13]

The arrangement worked well for the next 13 years, but by 2002, MCL&GL was in dire financial straits. One reason was the usurious publisher price increases (see Chapter 1). Another was that many lawyers had canceled their memberships, preferring to use Westlaw or LexisNexis. PLCMC considered a plan to buy the collection, contributing $25,000 to its upkeep for each of 4 years before taking it over in the fifth year, but this arrangement proved unworkable.[14] In 2003, PLCMC withdrew its support, leaving the law library a shell of itself.

It did not close, however. In 2005, I became its director, and I tried everything to save it—brochures, promotions, cost-cutting, membership discounts, publicity events. I begged for county and state funds, wrote grant applications, and asked every agency in Charlotte about a possible partnership. No one came forward to help. Finally, the board of directors sold the 22,000-plus volumes to the new Charlotte School of Law. After selling the collection and laying off the staff—me and two part-timers—the board dissolved itself with a letter to the North Carolina Secretary of State. That was the end of an 80-year institution.

Law firm libraries have suffered from shrinkage as well. In 1995, Baker & McKenzie, one of the world's largest law firms, made headlines by firing the 10-person staff in its Chicago headquarters library. The firm reasoned that outsourcing its collection maintenance to a law library vendor (see Chapter 4) would be cheaper. Plus, with Westlaw and LexisNexis at every attorney's fingertips, who needed professional researchers?[15] Four years later, it was *déjà vu* all over again as Pillsbury Madison & Sutro, a San Francisco firm, hired an independent contractor to handle its library operations. In 2003, the Fortune 500 company I worked for laid me off as the opening act of its law department library demolition. I ended up at a law firm whose spacious, skyline-view library (or so it was sometimes described) had been chopped and stuffed into an area half as big.

How can law libraries survive? They must adapt, something they are loath, yet well-suited, to do. Library services are an "open system," in the jargon of systems theory. "In other words," according to the scholar Michael Buckland, "activities that take place in the provision and use of library services are not isolated from the rest of the world."[16] Buckland goes on to say that

> [a]n important property of systems is their ability to respond to changes, to adapt themselves to their environments, and to maintain sufficient stability to survive. The characteristics of library services in this regard seem contradictory. Library services are generally regarded as being weak on the features needed for adaptation and stability—feedback on what is happening in library use is generally weak, incomplete, or lacking; the goals of library services are usually vague; library services are often criticized for being rather unresponsive; and librarians have little or no control over the environment. On the other hand, library services do exhibit some of the characteristics of systems that are adaptable: library services may have serious problems but rarely dramatic crises; and the popular stereotypic image of libraries is as safe, suitable places for timid persons to work rather than adventurous,

action-oriented "change agents." Even more significantly, library services do, in fact, *survive*. In other words, there is a paradox: library services do not appear to have the usual characteristics of adaptability, but they do share the crucial feature of adaptive systems—survival.[17]

In other words, law libraries must open themselves further. Historically, law libraries have focused on building collections, not doing outreach or creating innovative services. But innovation has become the watchword in legal research. Firms have embraced the digital world, but law schools still require students to use print materials for some projects. Public law libraries may provide access to legal databases, but most offer no training on how to use them. It would be a simple matter to hold one free public seminar per month on electronic legal research. Small firm attorneys would show up in droves, as would pro se litigants.

There is more to innovation, however, than a few seminars. Law libraries must *reinvent* their services.[18] For example, by partnering with state bar associations, libraries can host events such as North Carolina's 4ALL Statewide Service Day, when volunteer lawyers give free advice to anyone who calls.[19] The Clark County (WA) Law Library found new revenue sources by selling form packets, booklets, and notary services, while the Collin County (TX) Law Library began using the inmate commissary fund to support the jail library.[20] In Madison, Wisconsin, the Dane County Law Library transformed itself into the Dane County Legal Resource Center, collaborating with the county bar, small claims court, and other organizations to "meet user needs through the most useful resources and assistance."[21]

Law firm librarians need to innovate as well, starting with the way they are viewed. Librarians of old "took up the profession because they loved learning and they wanted to be of service to the common good. The work that went on in the library supported the firm's needs but often the work was done answering today's needs without thought to tomorrow."[22] Today's professionals must look at the library as a business-within-a-business. We are a *service* business, with strategic plans, revenue projections (see Chapter 8), and measures for success. The chief measure is customer satisfaction. "When we lost control of the mystery," writes one librarian, referring to patrons' ability to conduct their own research using the internet, "we became vulnerable to the classic problem of service entities: the customer does not always understand quality service or what is required to provide quality service."[23] For law firm librarians, this means constantly educating attorneys, paralegals, and other staff not just on the library's holdings, print and electronic, but on the capabilities of the library staff. Without this campaign, librarians "are in danger of being the next strike-through on a CFO's balance sheet."[24]

The good news is this: Law librarians are survivors. For generations, we have stayed vital to the profession, and as the practice of law changes, we innovate along with it. Yes, the headlines blare with law library closings, but not every institution is headed for shrinkage. In 2005, a major law firm in my city moved to a new building, where it constructed a *larger* library with *more* books. Law schools have expanded their libraries in recent years, and in 2013, in Houston, Texas, a new $600,000 county law library was opened, complete with a coffee bar, computer kiosks, and free legal services sponsored by the Houston Bar Association.[25]

Twelve years have passed since my first day at the library of Haynsworth Sinkler Boyd, and despite the struggles I have seen and been a part of, I have no regrets. Not one. The law is fascinating, and as a librarian, I stand at the t-junction of its past and future, ready to walk down any corridor to help my patrons. Sometimes I wonder what becomes of them. Do they get their expunctions, settle their custody arrangements, or win their lawsuits? Did Dan receive what he wanted from the North Carolina Right of Way Division? I guess I'll never know. All I can hope is that, if things didn't work out, he will come back to the library. I found a few *North Carolina Law Review* articles he will want to peruse.

Endnotes

1.   John P. Joergensen, "Deal or No Deal? Are LMAs Really in the Best Interest of law Librarians?" *AALL Spectrum* 15, no. 5 (March 2011): 13, 17.

2.   Richard A. Danner, Kelly Leong, and Wayne V. Miller, "The Durham Statement Two Years Later: Open Access in the Law School Journal Environment," *Law Library Journal* 103, no. 1 (2011): 39–54.

3.   Ibid.

4.   Debbie Rabina, "Public Information for All: An Interview with Carl Malamud," *Library Journal*, November 1, 2010, accessed November 29, 2012, www.libraryjournal.com:80/lj/communitycopyrightfairuse/887221-420/public_information_for_all_an.html.csp.

5.   Ibid.

6.   A main source of law-related microfiche is the Law Library Microform Consortium. See www.llmc.com.

7.   Scott Stolley, "Corruption of Legal Research," *For The Defense* 39 (April 2004): 40.

8.   Hillary Baker, "Battling the Economic Bully: How Tough Times Are Affecting Law Libraries, and How You Can Fight Back," *AALL Spectrum* 13, no. 8 (June 2009): 15.

9.   Calvin Godfrey, "Law Library Checks Out," *Miami New Times*, October 18, 2007, accessed November 29, 2012, www.miaminewtimes.com/2007-10-18/news/law-library-checks-out.

10. Francesca Jarosz, "Budget Cuts Force Law Library to Close," *Indianapolis Star*, January 2, 2010, accessed November 29, 2012, tinyurl.com/ccaxxvq.

11. Christian Nolan, "April Comes, and 3 Conn. Law Libraries Close," *Connecticut Law Tribune*, February 24, 2013, accessed April 5, 2010, tinyurl.com/d4d8mhe.

12. Deborah S. Panella, *Basics of Law Librarianship* (Binghamton, NY: Haworth Press, 1991), 2.

13. This arrangement is detailed in a Memorandum of Understanding dated December 6, 1990 between PLCMC and MCL&GL.

14. Michele Wayman, "Funding Crunch May Imperil Public Law Library; Drop in Memberships by Lawyers Puts Burden on City-County System," *Charlotte Observer*, September 22, 2002.
15. Apparently, Baker & McKenzie did, hiring a new library staff within 2 years.
16. Michael Buckland, *Library Services in Theory and Context*, 2nd ed. (Berkeley, CA: SunSITE, 1999), accessed November 29, 2012, sunsite. berkeley.edu/Literature/Library/Services/index.html.
17. Ibid.
18. Baker, "Battling the Economic Bully," 15.
19. Russell Rawlings, "4ALL Statewide Service Day Record-Setting Success," *NCBA News*, March 4, 2011, accessed November 29, 2012, www.ncbar.org/about/communications/news/2011-news-articles/ 4all-statewide-service-day-record-setting-success.aspx.
20. Paula Seeger, "Finding Hope in Funding Shortfalls," *AALL Spectrum* 12, no. 6 (April 2008): 22–25.
21. Ibid.
22. "The Future of Law Firm Libraries," Strategic Librarian, (blog), July 22, 2007, accessed November 29, 2012, www.strategiclibrarian.com/ 2007/07/22/the-future-of-law-firm-libraries.
23. Kay Moller Todd, "Law Firm Libraries in the 21st Century," *AALL Spectrum* 10, no. 9 (July 2006): 12.
24. Ibid.
25. Mike Morris, "County Law Library Gets New Look, Amenities," *Houston Chronicle*, November 26, 2012, accessed February 25, 2013, www.chron.com/news/houston-texas/houston/article/County-law-library-gets-new-look-amenities-4065719.php.

Appendix A

Patron Requests in Law Libraries

Included in this appendix are three sets of actual patron reference questions compiled in law libraries. One is from the Mecklenburg County Law & Government Library in Charlotte, North Carolina, where I worked in 2005 (see Chapter 10). The second is from the Washington County (OR) Law Library, available at www.co. washington.or.us/LawLibrary/upload/AALL_Sample_Reference_ Questions_-July09_June10.pdf. Finally, I threw in a few questions from one of the law firms I have served.

My thoughts on how some of these questions should be handled are in the Endnotes to this appendix.

Mecklenburg County Law & Government Library

1. I need a sample separation agreement.

2. I need to see the statute and sample form to file a lien.

3. Can you give me information on structured sentencing for misdemeanors?

4. Is it legal to shoot a BB gun in the city limits?[1]

5. What are the legal issues surrounding oral agreements?

6. How do I legitimize a child born out of wedlock?

7. I need to know the duties and responsibilities of the board of directors for a private corporation.

8. How do I form a nonprofit corporation?

9. How can my son get a crime expunged from his record?[2]

10. I need to appeal the decision on my unemployment claim.[3]

11. There is a law review article from the 1940s that is not on LexisNexis. Do you have a copy?[4]

12. I am trying to become a member of the Texas bar. Do you have Martindale-Hubbell directories back to 1996 showing that I was listed as a North Carolina attorney?[5]

13. My employer fired me for no reason. How can I sue them?[6]

14. I just lost my case in small claims court, and I want to appeal to district court. Where are the forms to do that?

15. What is the statute of limitations on medical malpractice cases in North Carolina?

16. How do I file a Freedom of Information Act request?

17. I am a CPA needing to research new tax law changes.

18. Are North Carolina Industrial Commission reports on the internet?[7]

19. Where do I go to report a worthless check?

20. I need help drafting a quitclaim deed.[8]

21. I need a sample form for transferring my interest in a partnership to someone else.

22. What are the laws in North Carolina regulating neighborhood associations?

23. I am thinking about going to law school, and I need information on school addresses and rankings.[9]

24. What are the elements of cocaine possession, and what class felony is it?

25. Where can I get a vehicle accident report off the internet?[10]

26. How do I file a complaint against a local judge?

27. I need some sample rental property management contracts.[11]

28. Where do I find bankruptcy in the *U.S. Code*?

29. How do I legally change my name?

30. I need some cases in which federal district courts have granted writs of prohibition.

Washington County (OR) Law Library

1. What do we have on probate for a criminal defense attorney?

2. I have to fill out custody forms; do you have any information on that?

3. Request for sample civil jury instructions.

4. I am looking for the bio on a lawyer who graduated from law school in 1933.[12]

5. Looking for a 2003 superseded ORS section.[13]

6. "No appeal certification" – how to get one?

7. Contempt of child custody agreement – Oregon laws and cases that are applicable.

8. Are there any legal requirements that a towing company has to follow concerning notifying owner of imminent towing?

9. How can I find motions (preferable for Wash. Co. Circuit Court) for ORCP 21?[14]

10. Legal definition of a word.

11. Guardianship materials.

12. Death and survivors.

13. I want to [know] my rights as a renter.

14. I got served papers for the disillusionment of my marriage. How do I respond? Am I responding to the marriage or custody issues?[15]

15. Do we have 1962 ORS?

16. Phone number for Beaverton Public Library

17. When did ORCP 55(e) come into existence? Was it passed after 1956?[16]

18. Law re: contractor's 'implied warranty' in the state of Washington.

19. How much do I owe on a ticket (not sure if OSP or Sheriff)? Don't have the ticket.

20. Do we have digital briefs from 2008?[17]

21. Do you have forms that I can use to file a complaint?[18]

22. How can I find out how much I owe for a seat belt violation ticket that I lost?

23. How to find active duty military status.

24. Notary available?

25. Do you have computers to do the child support calculators like they do in Multnomah Co. Law Library?[19]

26. Will Legal Aid Services be able to tell us if the government can represent me because we are disabled?

27. Need copy of 1973 Senate Bill 100.[20]

28. Need recent LUBA reports.[21]

29. Do you have OSB member directories from 1990 forward?

30. I need to check my work against a lawyer's handbook on guardianship.

31. Resources for the mentally disabled with discriminatory matters (church/school).

32. How do I get Oregon appellate court briefs?[22]

33. Legislative History – help in finding an effective date.[23]

34. What are my rights as a beneficiary?

35. I need a family law form pertaining to a divorce.[24]

36. We need to evict our son. What do we have to do and what can we do with his belongings?

37. What does our Westlaw subscription include?

38. Need a Nevada Revised Statute.[25]

39. What's the term for cancelling a signature on a contract you signed but didn't understand?[26]

40. How to defend civilly against case where you've been accused of improper behavior with a child?

41. Looking for the definitions to "right of way" and "permanent easement" as they pertain to land use.[27]

42. Materials for how to file an answer to a Federal Civil Complaint (labor law).

43. History of an administrative rule.[28]

44. Research materials on RICO.

45. How do I appeal a decision from an administrative judge (pro se)?

Law Firm

1. Here's the issue: Can an attorney licensed in state A defend a resident of state A at a deposition held in state A in a lawsuit filed and pending in state B? In other words, whereas the attorney clearly couldn't defend a deposition in state B—because she's not licensed there—could she nevertheless defend a deposition in state A that's pending elsewhere?[29]

2. I'm answering some questions a client has about the recent amendment to the South Carolina Constitution eliminating the "minibottle" requirement. Specifically, I'm researching the South Carolina statutes and regs, and I've found that the statutory amendments from June 2005 are available, but it doesn't look like the administrative code and regs have amendments (there are still references to "minibottles" in the regs, whereas the statutory provisions have been changed to "by the drink"). Is this the most recent version of the code? Also, if you could offer any other sources to assist me in my research, I'd greatly appreciate it!

3. Would you be able to get me a profile on this judge? He is a U.S. District Court judge in the Eastern District of North Carolina.

4. Can you send me the Macmillan case which is at 559 A.2d somewhere in the p. 1260 range and the Kahn case at 694 A.2d somewhere in the p. 429 range?[30]

5. Could you obtain copies of the following? Thanks.

   • National Aviation Corp., 23 S.E.C. 309 (1946)

   • Bankers National Investing Corp., IC-385/386 (1942)

   • Value Line Special Situations Fund, Inc., IC-8044/8089 (1973)

- Capital Administration Co., 34 S.E.C. 735 (1953)

- E. I. du Pont de Nemours & Co., IC-6083 (1970)[31]

6. Please do a search to see what articles/documents/ studies you come up with on the University of Pittsburgh's "recently" published study regarding hydrogen sulfide and also whatever information you can find on the actual studies by American researchers Dr. Richard Axel and Linda B. Buck (winners of the 2004 Nobel Prize in physiology or medicine) regarding smell and the human nose. Finally, there's an article that's been published in the Special Asphalt Issue of the *American Journal of Industrial Medicine* Vol. 43 No. 1 regarding a 2003 study of multicountry asphalt workers.[32]

7. Will you please get me a current address (do a "locator search") for

- Thomas Cheek

- 08/10/45

- Route 1, Box 65

- Milo, MO 64767 (We are trying to sue this guy and need information for service and the complaint)[33]

8. Do you know how to get sample interrogatories from the free Bender database in a personal injury case? Bender has a personal injury directory/database, and they've got lots of stuff about interrogatories. However, what I've found is pretty general. I'd like to know if they have actual suggested language for interrogatories in an injury case (re: damages, experts, lost earnings, etc.).[34]

9. Pls get asap a copy of this article for me: Daniel E. Troy, FDA Involvement in Product Liability Lawsuits, FDLI Update, Jan–Feb 2003.[35]

10. In a nutshell, the patron wants to know if you can obtain a copy of the episode of the soap opera *Guiding Light* that aired on August 3, 1998. Believe it or not, this relates to a product liability case (it's not for his personal enjoyment!).[36]

Endnotes

1. A fabulous resource for city and county ordinances is www.muni code.com. Of course, it does not cover every city and county in the U.S. For smaller entities, check the main county library.
2. This is one of the most common requests. It is also generally one of the easiest, as the state statutes will usually spell out the procedure.
3. This is a tricky request. Since this person is really asking *how* to do something, it is easy to stray into unauthorized practice of law.
4. A reason not to throw out all those old journal issues!
5. What did I tell you about keeping old copies of the *Martindale-Hubbell Law Directory*?
6. This is another procedural question. It is best to refer questions like these to a do-it-yourself book like the type published by Nolo Press (see Chapter 9).
7. Indeed they are, though only from the 1990s. See www.ic.nc.gov/database.html.
8. This is another person asking how to do something. I would find a form in a series like *AmJur Legal Forms* and let the patron figure it out himself.
9. A great place for this is the National Association of Legal Professionals Directory of Law Schools, available at www.nalplaw schoolsonline.org.
10. Nowhere, unless you pay for it through a public records database (see Chapter 7), to which the general public typically does not have access.
11. Another job for *AmJur Legal Forms* or a similar forms series.
12. Another reason to keep old copies of *Martindale-Hubbell*, though no library would have the space or fortitude to maintain an 80-year-old copy.
13. ORS = Oregon Revised Statutes. *The Bluebook* is a fabulous resource for identifying abbreviations.
14. ORCP = Oregon Rules of Civil Procedure. Also indentified using *The Bluebook*.

15. Here is another plea for help. Divorce and child custody questions are among the most common—and the most emotional. Usually, the requester has gotten the runaround from the courts and any number of attorneys, and he or she is stressed to the breaking point. Handle these questions with extra caution.

16. A legislative history question, often handled by consulting an annotated code (see Chapter 2).

17. This question is not about undergarments but electronic copies of appellate court filings (briefs). See Chapter 7.

18. Though there are form books like *AmJur Legal Forms*, these are really collections of templates. When a patron asks for a "form," what he really wants is something to fill out, check off, and submit, like an IRS form. The courts do not work that way. To file a complaint, which is the beginning of a lawsuit, there is no standard form; you have to draft the complaint yourself based on the specifics of your case. It is hard to explain this to patrons.

19. Resist the urge to reply, "Well, why don't you just go to Multnomah County Law Library?"

20. This is another legislative history question.

21. *The Bluebook* won't help you with this one. LUBA means Oregon's Land Use Board of Appeals. This is one you would know through experience or using Google. Or you could try *Prince's Bieber Dictionary of Legal Abbreviations*, published by William S. Hein (www.wshein.com).

22. A research guide on this topic is available at www.co.washington.or.us/LawLibrary/upload/Briefs_HowtoFind-2.pdf.

23. Yet *another* legislative history question. Legislative history is a big part of a law librarian's job that I simply can't cover in detail in this book. A good source for learning more is LLSDC's Legislative Source Book (www.llsdc.org/sourcebook).

24. Another request for an IRS-like form. You would have to explain to this patron that the court system does not work like that.

25. This is like saying, "I need a North Carolina case." If you must laugh, laugh on the inside.

26. This is called a "rescission." *Black's Law Dictionary* is the perfect tool for this request.

27. Dan the Day Laborer strikes again!

28. For history of a regulation, you will have to trace it through the *Federal Register* (for a U.S. reg) or the state equivalent (for a state reg).

29.   As you can see, attorney requests are typically more detailed and specific than those from the general public. Then again, what with "state A" and "state B," I remember feeling less informed after reading the question than before.

30.   This is an example of the "wrong or incomplete citations" you are liable to get from attorneys (see Chapter 3).

31.   These may not be "wrong or incomplete citations," but they are obscure ones. The first place to start, of course, is *The Bluebook*. If that doesn't work, then move on to *Prince's Bieber Dictionary of Legal Abbreviations*. I had trouble finding some of these, and when I asked the requester for more information, he replied, "The treatise I'm referring to uses the cites I gave you." Remarkably, authors of treatises don't always format citations correctly. In these situations, I might search for the citations in the law journals database on Westlaw or LexisNexis (see Chapter 5). Another writer might have cited the same documents more clearly.

32.   This is a good example of the nonlegal research law firm librarians have to do. This request came from one of the environmental law paralegals.

33.   I got questions like this all the time. See Chapter 7 for information on locating individuals.

34.   "Bender" refers to Matthew Bender, a treatise publisher owned by LexisNexis. Matthew Bender does have a general interrogatories treatise, but sometimes specialty treatises work better. I sent this requester to a West title, *Stein on Personal Injury Damages*, which had exactly what he was looking for.

35.   At the time, this article was not available on Westlaw, LexisNexis, or any other database our library subscribed to. It was also not available free on the internet. The Georgetown University library had hard copies of the journal, and I was able to get the article copied and emailed to me.

36.   In 12 years of law librarianship, this is my most fabulous research request. I started with the CBS network, but it did not provide copies of individual episodes. Next I tried a few television archives (e.g., the Museum of Broadcast Communications in Chicago), to no avail. Finally, I asked myself, who is the most likely type of person to have this information? Answer: a fan of the show. This led me to soap opera discussion boards. I did not find the episode, but that is because the attorney called off the search after a day or two. I think I could have found it if I had kept at it on the discussion boards.

Appendix B

Library Business Case

Business Case for a Managed Program
for Legal Research and Writing

Presented to
Members of the Expanded Staff
Office of General Counsel
ABC Corporation

Prepared by
The Operations Team
Office of General Counsel
ABC Corporation

2003

Executive Summary

The purpose of this business case is to recommend a managed program for legal research and writing for the ABC Corporation Office of General Counsel (OGC). The objectives of this program include:

- Reducing overall spending of the OGC on research and writing (estimated at $7–9 million annually) while maintaining the quality of work

- Making budgeting easier by using the fixed-fee services of a specialized research vendor

- Avoiding duplication of work by storing existing research memoranda in an electronic database

The program has three components. Due to the potential for immediate savings (up to $2.25 million annually), the Operations team recommends adopting all three components now. They are:

1. Establishing a business relationship between the OGC and a vendor that specializes in legal research and writing

2. Creating the role of "research director" and making that person responsible for managing the OGC's research agenda

3. Developing an electronic database that will house OGC work product and make it available for re-use

If we do not rely on software already owned by OGC for the third component, then the Operations team recommends delaying that step for 1 year due to the cost of purchasing new software.

Background

Research is the bedrock of legal advice. It is a competency that should be managed like any other element of practicing law. Unfortunately, most corporate law departments do not take advantage of current best practices. In-house attorneys, paralegals, and their assistants cannot research and write on all the issues they encounter daily. Moreover, heady law firm costs *vis-à-vis* the inexperience of junior attorneys who do most of the research and writing at those firms make it necessary to explore better avenues.

On the basis of this idea, the Operations team researched industry practices and talked to members of the OGC to arrive at a description of how legal research is handled. At ABC Corporation, the current process for assigning research projects is as follows:

1. Telephone discussion of research need between law firm partner and in-house attorney

2. Conference(s) between law firm partner who will manage the research and law firm associate(s) who will conduct it

3. Hours of research and writing by associate(s)

4. Review of draft memorandum or brief by law firm partner

5. Revisions and possible second review by partner

6. Delivery of final document to in-house attorney

All the time that the law firm commits to this process is billed to OGC. Invoices also include overhead costs that the firm can pass along—photocopies, long distance phone calls, postage, and computer-assisted research (a capability that we already have). In addition, we may not receive copies of what law firm attorneys write as an outgrowth of their research, raising the question of how we assess the efforts that undergird our representation—groundwork that is not cheap.

For example, from June 2002 to December 2002, a sample of 14 OGC attorneys approved invoices containing roughly $524,985 for legal research and writing.[1] It seems likely, then, that the entire OGC (80-plus attorneys) spent $7–9 million for the year on those tasks alone. This is consistent with industry reports suggesting that 6–20 percent of a corporate law department's outside counsel expenses go to research and writing.[2]

Discussion

Legal Research Vendor

Over the last 3 decades, companies specializing in legal research and writing have sprung up.[3] Their employees are legal experts, not fledgling associates, and they work in conjunction with networks of independent contractors consisting of law professors and former practitioners who bring years of theoretical amplitude and practice experience. DuPont, Prudential, Motorola, State Farm, and Johnson & Johnson are some of the U.S. companies that have hired a vendor to handle their research and writing needs.

In search of a way to make research management part of OGC's aggressive plan to reduce outside counsel costs in 2003, the Operations team began talking to a pair of these vendors. Their presentations and third-party acclaim of their business model led to the consideration of a long-term relationship with one or both of them as a cheaper alternative to outside counsel. In time, this idea became part of a larger plan to make legal research and writing a process that could be unbundled (to some extent) and managed, resulting in significant savings. According to our inquiries, California-based Legal Research Network (LRN) and Minnesota-based Legal Research Center (LRC) seem to be the industry leaders.

These vendors use a different process than outside counsel. After an initial call to define the project, the vendors develop a blueprint for the proposed research and quote a price. The price varies by number of jurisdictions, number of legal issues, tone of the final memo (objective versus persuasive), turnaround time, and specialty area. Research is done according to client specifications and delivered via email, fax, or overnight carrier. Some projects can be completed within 48 hours. More complex assignments take 10–14 business days. The vendors prefer to collaborate with a company's outside counsel, but, in some instances, they may substitute for legal research normally conducted by in-house attorneys and paralegals (see Figure B.1 on page 224 for a map of the research process).

The benefits of a relationship with one of these vendors are conspicuous. The biggest benefit is the potential savings. As a test, the Operations team hired a vendor to write a memo on an issue that a law firm had researched in 2002. The firm's memo cost $4,200; the vendor's price was $3,500 (a 17 percent savings). For two other projects, OGC paid law firms $3,991 and $5,600; the vendor quoted prices of $2,150 (47 percent savings) and $2,400 (58 percent savings), respectively, to do the same work. Several sources indicate that using a research vendor can save up to 25 percent of a law department's research budget,[4] which could work out to savings of $2.25 million a year for OGC. Table B.1 summarizes other benefits.

Table B.1   Other Benefits of Using a Research Vendor

Project Characteristic	Outside Counsel	Research Vendor
Research sources	Junior associate or paralegal	Experienced practitioner
Cost per project	Number of hours x billing rate	Flat fee (usually $5,000–$10,000)
Money-back guarantee	No	Yes
Additional work or staff needed	OGC pays	Absorbed by vendor
Hidden costs	Phone calls, copies, Westlaw or LexisNexis access fees	None
Volume discounts	Sometimes	Always

The General Counsel Roundtable reports the following feedback from its members on their use of research vendors:

- Some uneven experience with the vendor, but members note that its services improve as the relationship lengthens.

- Vendors excel at 50-state surveys and employment topics, but their work on tax issues is less satisfactory.

- Based on quantitative analysis of risk and cost data, the net benefit of engaging a vendor is positive.

- Nearly all members currently using research vendors recommend their services.[5]

Research Director

The OGC can reap savings, take advantage of internet-driven trends, and enhance the law department's work by assigning central responsibility for legal research management to an in-house research director. The duties of the research director would include:

- Advising OGC attorneys on the most cost-effective avenue for completing research projects

- Consulting with outside counsel on significant research and writing assignments

- Managing OGC's relationship with the research vendor

- Incorporating work product into a knowledge database

- Training others to use the database

- Using knowledge management (KM) principles to create an information-rich culture in the OGC

Other companies (e.g., the Xerox Corporation) have created similar positions and have been pleased with the results. Obvious benefits include:

- Realizing immediate savings

- Having a central contact who can explore methods of using technology to reduce legal research costs and manage relationships with legal research and writing vendors

- Developing legal research and writing as an area of in-house expertise

Knowledge Database

Any research vendor would give all the documents it writes to the OGC. With these added to memoranda written in-house or by outside counsel, we would be able to create a knowledge database. Then, when research is needed, we or our law firm partners could search the database for an existing memo to adapt, which might

Table B.2   Benefits of the Knowledge Database System

Concern	Without Database	With Database
Boundaries	Knowledge sharing among attorneys awkward	None
Attrition	Legal knowledge leaves with attorneys	Legal knowledge remains
Search	Hard to uncover relevant prior work product	Prior work product easily identified
Redundancies	Common	Rare
Quality	Uneven	Enhanced by access to prior work product
Speed	Attorneys start from scratch	Attorneys have advantaged starting point

eliminate the need for new research. Table B.2 summarizes the benefits of this system.

We could create this database at any time through existing technology or at an additional cost from a research vendor. While a database is a goal of this business case, additional cost–benefit analysis will determine the most appropriate method to establish it.

Research Process

Ideally, OGC attorneys could assign some issues to the research vendor via the research director and use the results to form a legal opinion. This method is especially useful for routine matters and "lay of the law" questions such as a 50-state survey. Other matters are too complex or sensitive for this type of disposition. Outside counsel will need to remain involved in these matters, but we can stipulate that the law firm will direct the "pure" research—defining terms, analyzing states and cases, and discussing options—to the research vendor. The vendor would then return a summary of the research findings to outside counsel, who would use those findings to inform their opinion to us. Figure B.1 illustrates the process.

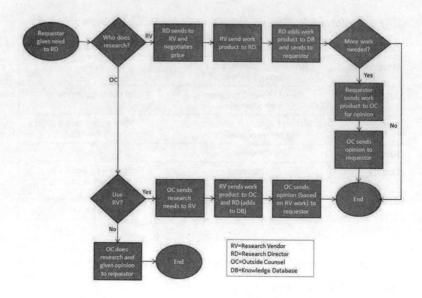

Figure B.1   Research process

Challenges

To make this program work, some aspects of our current model will have to change:

- Unbundling, at least so far as research and writing are concerned, will have to become a way of doing business.

- OGC attorneys must be willing to share all research needs with the research director and frame research questions clearly.

- Outside counsel must be willing to work with the research director and accept the work of the research vendor.

Nevertheless, the opportunity to save the OGC up to $2.25 million a year argues in favor of adopting the program.

Conclusion

On the basis of this discussion, the Operations team recommends:

- Establishing a business relationship between the OGC and a vendor that specializes in legal research and writing

- Appointing an OGC research director to manage the department's research activities

- Developing a knowledge database to house work product written for OGC by the research vendor and outside counsel alike

The research director will lead OGC efforts during the inaugural phase and will remain an important advocate for a first-rate research process beyond that period.

The benefits are clear. The virtuosity of the experts available to the research vendor will be a welcome addition to the OGC's team of partners as it delivers high-quality work. Outside counsel can devote less time to research, which is not its core competency, and more time to the tasks it does well. Using previous work product from the knowledge database will curtail duplication and keep us from losing legal knowledge when our teammates move on to different demands. Finally, the OGC can trim as much as $2.25 million off its cost of doing business—a feat that upholds our standard of accountability and reinforces our role as advisors, experts, and leaders.

Endnotes

1. We arrived at this estimate by adding line items in paid OGC invoices that were clearly associated with research and writing. The actual amount spent is undoubtedly higher because some invoices were not reviewed and others were too esoteric to make research costs identifiable.
2. Robert L. Haig, ed., *Successful Partnering Between Inside and Outside Counsel* (Eagan, MN: West Group, 2000), § 19:2.

3. Lisa Stansky, "Going Outside for Legal Research," *National Law Journal*, August 26, 2002.

4. Haig, *Successful Partnering*, § 19:2; Mark Ohringer and Bill Moss, "Legal Knowledge Management Yields Corporate Rewards," *Metropolitan Corporate Counsel*, December 2001; Krysten Crawford, "Finding a Way Out of the Pyramid," *The Recorder*, July 22, 1996.

5. General Counsel Roundtable, *Compendium of Cost Savings Tactics* (Washington, DC: Corporate Executive Board, 2002).

About the Author

Anthony Aycock became a librarian in 2001. Since then, he has worked at a law school, two major law firms, a corporate legal department, and various public libraries. He has a BA in English, an MLIS, an MFA in creative writing, and a master's in criminal justice. Anthony has published essays and articles in the *Missouri Review*, *Gettysburg Review*, *Creative Nonfiction*, *ONLINE*, *Library Journal*, *National Paralegal Reporter*, and *Community & Junior College Libraries*. This is his first book.

From 1992 to 2000, Anthony worked as a McDonald's restaurant manager. He has only two things to say about that career: (1) Big Mac sauce is not Thousand Island dressing; and (2) the next time you use a drive-thru in the rain, please, please turn off your windshield wipers at the pay window.

Index

appellate briefs, reasons for
obtaining, 150
appellate cases, xv, 9, 25, 121, 127,
150–151
articles
American Law Reports annotations, 32
in bar association journals, 37
debate about, 15–16
encyclopedia, 31
on law firm management, 119
on law librarianship, 18, 181,
197
medical, 148–149
news, 63
newsletter, 84
articles, finding legal
journal, 35, 38, 113
via ABA Free Full-Text Online
Law Review/Journal
Search, 194
via Google Scholar, 127
via HeinOnline, 35, 113
via Legal News Reader, 132
via LegalTrac, 115
via mobile apps, 131
via U.S. Code, 23
via Westlaw or LexisNexis, 12,
35, 92, 99, 108, 113
associations, law library/librarian,
189–190
Atlantic Digest, 41
Atlantic Reporter, 11
attorneys
blogs by, 184–185, 186
litigation, 171
need for legal research, 138
referrals to, 53
research by, importance, 46–47
responsibilities, 22
use of legal materials, 10–12, 15,
16, 34–35, 195
use of mobile devices, 128

atVantage tool for business development, 158
Authenticity Consulting Free
Management Library,
160–161
Aycock, Anthony, xvii–xviii, xix, 71,
77–78, 183–184

B

Baker & McKenzie (law firm), 102,
104, 200–201
Balleste, Roy, 172–173
bankruptcy cases, 127, 143
Bankruptcy Law Reporter, 84, 85
bar associations
American, 16, 36–37, 128, 170
attorney referrals, 53
law journals, 36–37, 115, 131,
194, 198
publications, 36–37, 52
state/local, 37, 52
Basics of Law Librarianship
(Panella & Mount), xix, 172
Bender's Federal Practice Forms, 9
beSpacific (blog), 181
Better Business Bureau (BBB)
Reviews (website), 143
Big Charts (website), 140
billing
clients for database access, 93,
101, 102–103, 105, 106
for reference services, 64, 155
tools for establishing rates, 133
binders, looseleaf, 72, 73, 80, 81
Bintliff, Barbara, 173–174
Bizarre Questions and What
Library School Never Taught
You (website), 45
bizarre questions from patrons,
45–46, 60–61
Blackburn, Sharon, 61

indexes
  collections of, 116
  law journals, 35
  LegalTrac as, 115
  looseleaf, 73, 75
  newsletter, 86
  statutory codes, 24
  use in research, 91, 98
IndexMaster, 116
Index to Legal Periodicals, 35
individuals people, researching.
    See people, researching
    individual
inexperienced researchers, work-
    ing with, 65–66
information, right to, 197
InfoTrac, 115. *See also* LegalTrac
    database
inquiries, patron. *See* reference,
    legal
insane patrons, 61
interference, 168–169
interfiled looseleafs, 73–74
international information, avail-
    ability, 115, 116, 119, 179,
    198
international legal journals, 115
Introduction to Basic Legal
    Citation (website), 52
Investing in Bonds (website), 141
I Want Media (website), 141

J

James Publishing, 9
JD degree, 169–171
Jesus photo question, 45–46
Jobs, Steve, 5
John Wiley & Sons (publisher), 15
John Wiley Law Publications (pub-
    lisher), 7
Jones McClure (publisher), 9

journals, law. *See also* law reviews
  attorney use, 195
  bar association, 36–37, 115, 131,
    194, 198
  database availability, 113, 115
  finding articles, 35–38, 113
  history, 13–16
  indexes, 35
  international, 115
  mobile access, 131
  publication format, 194–195
  sources, 15, 113, 115, 127, 131,
    194–195
journals, medical, 148, 149
J-STOR, 35
judgment, xiv
Judiciary Act (1789), 47
Justia (website), 195

K

Kennedy, Justice Anthony, 15
Kent, James, 4
KeyCite, 29, 38, 96–97, 103–104,
    129
key numbers, case
  described, 6
  learning, 188
  LexisNexis, 99
  West, 26, 27, 28, 93–94, 95
keyword searches, 51–52, 65, 91,
    169. *See also* Google search
    tool
King County, Seattle collection
    development policy, 17
knowledge, right to, 196–197
Krause, Margaret, 159–160
Kroc, Ray, 5

More Great Books from Information Today, Inc.

The Accidental Systems Librarian, 2nd Ed.

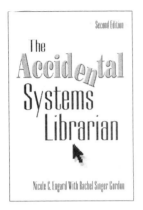

By Nicole C. Engard with Rachel Singer Gordon

This new edition of *The Accidental Systems Librarian* prepares readers to manage the latest library technologies: mobile devices, open source software, social networks, WiFi, ebooks, and much more. Nicole C. Engard's advice on using research, communication, organizational, and bibliographic skills to solve various systems problems is geared to helping both "accidental" and "planned" systems librarians develop the skills they need to succeed and the confidence they need to excel.

328 pp/softbound/ISBN 978-1-57387-453-3 $29.50
Ebook also available

The Accidental Health Sciences Librarian

By Lisa A. Ennis and Nicole Mitchell

Sparked by an aging baby boomer population, the dizzying pace of breakthroughs in medical research, and an unprecedented proliferation of health information, you may soon discover a career opportunity in health sciences librarianship. Lisa A. Ennis and Nicole Mitchell offer a thorough and up-to-date overview along with guidance on a range of critical resources, tools, and functions. Their coverage of such essential topics as HIPAA and MeSH, along with a wealth of expert tips and advice, is a must for all new, prospective, and working health sciences librarians.

232 pp/softbound/ISBN 978-1-57387-395-6 $29.50
Ebook also available

The Accidental Taxonomist

By Heather Hedden

The Accidental Taxonomist is the most comprehensive guide available to the art and science of building information taxonomies. Heather Hedden walks readers through the process, displaying her trademark ability to present highly technical information in straightforward, comprehensible English. Drawing on numerous real-world examples, Hedden explains how to create terms and relationships, select taxonomy management software, design taxonomies for human versus automated indexing, manage enterprise taxonomy projects, and adapt taxonomies to various user interfaces. The result is a practical and essential guide for information professionals who need to effectively create or manage taxonomies, controlled vocabularies, and thesauri.

472 pp/softbound/ISBN 978-1-57387-397-0 $39.50
Ebook also available

The Accidental Library Marketer

By Kathy Dempsey

The Accidental Library Marketer fills a need for library professionals and paraprofessionals who find themselves in an awkward position: They need to promote their libraries and services in the age of the internet, but they've never been taught how to do it effectively. This results-oriented A-to-Z guide by Kathy Dempsey reveals the missing link between the everyday promotion librarians actually do and the "real marketing" that's guaranteed to assure funding, excite users, and build stronger community relationships. Combining real-life examples, expert advice, and checklists in a reader-friendly style, this is the complete how-to resource for successful library marketing and promotion.

312 pp/softbound/ISBN 978-1-57387-368-0 $29.50
Ebook also available

The Embedded Librarian
Innovative Strategies for Taking Knowledge
Where It's Needed

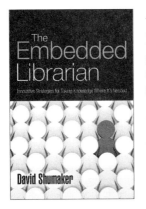

By David Shumaker

Here is the first comprehensive survey of the growing practice of "embedded librarianship"— a strategic model for placing information professionals into partnerships with the individuals and working groups that depend upon their knowledge and expertise. David Shumaker looks at implementations in all types of organizations, identifies the characteristics of successful embedded librarians, and explains how information professionals in public, academic, school, medical, law, and other specialized library settings enhance their careers.

232 pp/softbound/ISBN 978-1-57387-452-6 $49.50
Ebook also available

The Librarian's Guide to Negotiation
Winning Strategies for the Digital Age

By Beth Ashmore, Jill E. Grogg, and Jeff Weddle

This practical guide provides an in-depth look at negotiation in theory and practice, share tactics and strategies of top negotiators, offer techniques for overcoming emotional responses to conflict, recall successful outcomes and deals gone awry, and demonstrate the importance of negotiating expertise to libraries and library careers. The result is an eye-opening survey into the true nature of negotiation—both as a form of communication and as a tool you can use to create sustainable collections and improve library service in the digital age.

264 pp/softbound/ISBN 978-1-57387-428-1 $49.50
Ebook also available

Web of Deceit
Misinformation and Manipulation in the
Age of Social Media

Edited by Anne P. Mintz

For all its benefits, the worldwide social media phenomenon has provided manipulative people and organizations with the tools that allow hoaxes and con games to be perpetrated on a vast scale. Anne P. Mintz brings together a team of experts to explain how misinformation is intentionally spread and to illuminate the dangers in a range of critical areas. *Web of Deceit* is a must-read for any internet user who wants to avoid being victimized.

320 pp/softbound/ISBN 978-0-910965-91-0 $29.95
Ebook also available

The Extreme Searcher's Internet Handbook, 4th Ed.

By Randolph Hock

The Extreme Searcher's Internet Handbook is the essential guide for anyone who uses the internet for research. In this fully updated fourth edition, Ran Hock covers strategies and tools for all major areas of internet content. Readers with little to moderate searching experience will appreciate Hock's helpful, easy-to-follow advice, while experienced searchers will discover a wealth of new techniques and resources.

344 pp/softbound/ISBN 978-1-937290-02-3 $24.95
Ebook also available